Analysis of J.S. Bach's Wohltemperirtes Clavier (48 Preludes & Fugues)

AUGENER'S EDITION, No. 9205

ANALYSIS

OF

J. S. BACH'S
Wohltemperirtes Clavier

(48 Preludes & Fugues)

BY

Dr. H. RIEMANN

h

TRANSLATED FROM THE GERMAN BY

J. S. SHEDLOCK, B.A.

PART I.
PRELUDES & FUGUES Nos. 1 to 24

FIFTH IMPRESSION

AUGENER Ltd.
LONDON

TO

Prof. Dr. PHILIPP SPITTA

THE ENTHUSIASTIC BIOGRAPHER

OF

J. S. BACH

Printed in England
by
AUGENER LTD.,
287 Acton Lane, London, W. 4.

CONTENTS.

(FIRST PART.)

PREFACE.

The present analysis of J. S. Bach's "Wohl-temperirtes Clavier" may be regarded as a sequel to the "Catechism of Composition", and specially as a Guide to fugal composition by the help of the most wonderful master-pieces in this branch of musical art; for to students of composition good examples are far more profitable than abstract rules and vague pre-scripts. If a well-known teacher of counterpoint is accustomed to tell his pupils that really not one of the fugues in the "Wohl. Clavier" is according to rule, surely one might turn the spit and maintain that rules which do not agree with Bach's fugues are worthless.

The first result of the present analysis of fugues is to establish in the clearest manner the perfect agreement of Bach's fugal structure with the norm of all other musical formation; tripartite division according to the scheme A—B—A (foundation-laying section in the principal key, modulating middle section, con-cluding section in the principal key is everywhere clearly exposed to view; and sound reasons, likewise, may be given for the few apparent exceptions. The free episodes are not merely connecting members inserted between the principal sections of the fugue, but they appear in the principal sections themselves, are complementary to the theme entries, serving as foils to them, or surpassing and crowning them. It is quite evident that such an exposition of the contra-diction between the fugal composition of the greatest master of fugue and pig-tail scholastic rules tends to excite strong opposition to insipid artificiality and formal workmanship, and opens up a path to youthful students in the practice of strict polyphonic com-position.

The analysis of the preludes must be regarded in the light of a supplement to my work. As the preludes stand in close spiritual relationship to the fugues, it seemed to me that I had to consider them with regard to their spiritual contents; the technical (harmonic-metrical) analysis will not, however, I trust, be without its use. The astonishing simplicity and strict logic of the harmonic and modulatory structure causes these pre-ludes to rank as truly classical models of development from short motives; future generations may study them again and again with profit. The harmonic schemes here communicated may be turned to most useful account if advanced readers try to work them out from figured bass at the pianoforte, but with other motives than those developed by Bach; the schemes may also be transposed and worked out in a similar manner, and the diversity of form which results, the utmost simplicity notwithstanding, will afford just cause for astonishment.

Sondershausen, June 15 1890.

Dr. Hugo Riemann.

PREFACE.

In order that the present analyses may be of service to those unacquainted with the other theoretical works of the author, it will be necessary first to offer a brief explanation of the harmony signs employed, as well as of the method of marking periods by figures beneath the bar strokes.

The new system of figuring chords traces back all harmony formations to the only two possible kinds of consonant chords, the Major and the Minor Chord, which are opposed the one to the other, and designated according to the doctrines of the greatest theorists of the past (Zarlino, Tartini, Moritz Hauptmann): — the Major Chord as the union of a note with those notes directly related to it above (prime, upper-third, upper-fifth), and the Minor Chord as the union of a note with those notes directly related to it below (prime, under-third, under-fifth). The intervals, considered upwards, of the Major Chord are indicated by *Arabian*, those, considered downwards, of the Minor Chord, by *Roman figures*, as for example: —

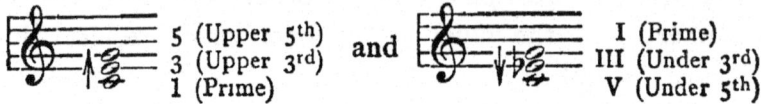

5 (Upper 5th)	I (Prime)
3 (Upper 3rd) and	III (Under 3rd)
1 (Prime)	V (Under 5th)

The Major Chord is briefly expressed by the *clang-letter* corresponding to its prime (*c, d, a* etc., or *c♯, d♯*, or *c♭, d♭*) with addition of a small *cross* +, which latter, however, when no misunderstanding is to be feared, can be omitted; the Minor Chord, likewise, is expressed by the *clang-letter* corresponding to its prime, with addition of a *nought* (o) in place of a +. The cross is really an abbreviation for $\frac{5}{3}$, the ° for $\frac{I}{III}$: both are therefore super-

fluous, when, for other reasons, figures become necessary
(for instance, when it has to be shown that the third is
in the bass, or when one of the three notes of the chord
requires chromatic alteration, or finally when other dis-
sonant notes are to be added to the chord); $\frac{\circ}{3}$, for instance
is the c Major Chord with the third as bass note; $g^{\triangleright}$ a
c Minor Chord (a g under-clang, or in short "under g")
with lowered prime ($g\flat$). The two signs $\prec$ (*raising* by a semitone) and $\succ$ (*lowering* by a semitone) constitute the remaining signs of this system. The *figures* 2, 4, 6, 7, 8 and 9
(likewise II, IV, VI, VII, VIII and IX) are employed
quite after the manner of general-bass figuring for the
intervals of the second, fourth, sixth, seventh, octave, ninth,
but always thought of from the prime (indicated by a
clang-letter) of a Major or Minor Chord; therefore, always
indicating an interval of definite size, as namely: — 1 (I)
always the unchanged prime, 3 (III) the (major) third,
5 (V) the perfect fifth of the chord, and

2 (II)	stands	for	the	major second
4 (IV)	„	„	„	perfect fourth
6 (VI)	„	„	„	major sixth
7 (VII)	„	„	„	minor (!) seventh
8 (VIII)	„	„	„	perfect octave = 1 (I)
9 (IX)	„	„	„	major ninth = 2 (II)
10 (X)	„	„	„	major tenth = 3 (III)

In some cases figures occur in combination with (but in
contradiction to) the clang signs (+, °), and then the clang
signs of the chord and the figure have, with regard to the
note, opposite meanings, for example $°a^{2\succ} = d$ Minor
Chord (minor chord under a, abbr. "under a") with suspension of the minor *upper* second of the prime, *i. e.*
$d\ f\ (a)\ b\flat$ (= chord of the Neapolitan 6th); also the

union of two kinds of figures occurs, for instance $\frac{e^7}{V}\ \frac{°e}{V}$ =

progression of the dominant chord with the seventh (e^7)
to the tonic $°e$ over the already anticipated fundamental

note of the tonic : the slur from the

one bass figure to the other is the convenient means adopted in *organ-point figuring*, for example g_1^6, f g^7 c d^+ g^7 c$^+$

When a figure has a *stroke* through it, this indicates the *omission* of the note represented by that figure: if the prime is to be left out, the clang letter has a stroke through it

$$f^6_3 = f\ a\ [c]\ d$$
$$g^7 = [g]\ b\ d\ f$$

Two points (..) indicate the repetition of the preceding harmony.

All the signs employed may be shown in an example, first written out with general-bass figuring

6♭	6♭	6♮	6♮	7	7 8	7♭	10	6
4		4♮	4	5	4 3			5
2♭	♭		3	♮	2 3		6	4 3
		3♮					♮	

The indications introduced by Gottfried Weber (1824), and adopted by F. Schneider, E. F. Richter and others, in which triads, chords of the seventh etc. are taken on the various degrees of the scale, can only with difficulty express this example

c: I ♭II⁷ | II⁰⁷ V⁺⁷ | ?I | ♯I⁰⁷⁰ II | V² | I
  G ♭V⁷ | I ♯V⁷ | V⁰⁷ | d: ♯VII⁷⁰ I | ♯III⁰⁷
       g: V⁷ | | | G: VII⁰⁷ ? I

Here is the new method of figuring, in which the progression of the bass is also partly indicated: —

c d♭ | g♭ d⁷ | c VII g♭⁷ | .. c | d⁹⁻ ⁰a | d⁹ g♭⁷ | c
    ⁷ | 3   5 | III | v 1 | | 6 5 |

Each sign contains a full explanation of the chord
For example g♭♭< .. c represents here a chord of domi-
        V ¹

nant seventh (g⁷) with augmented fifth (5<) passing over
the fundamental note of the tonic chord (..) to the same (c⁺).
                               (V)

The *Period of eight measures*, as normal formation,
is the basis of formal analysis: the measure (or bar in
the restricted sense for such counting) is therefore the formation consisting of two, likewise three beats or counts
of medium value (between 60 and 120 M. M.), compared
with which the composers' bar often appears too short
(for example in ³/₄ measure with tempo ♩. = 80), often
too long (compound, for example in ⁴/₄ measure with
♩ = 90).

This Period of eight measures, is formed by continued
symmetrical construction, beginning with the opposition
of 2 time-units of which the second answers to the first;
and thus already a first small symmetry (the measure) is
marked off

$$\frac{2}{4} \quad \overset{\smile}{\underset{1}{}} \ \Big| \ \overset{-}{\underset{2}{}}$$

This *accented* beat (the *answering* one) is somewhat
longer, and, as a rule, is given out with stronger production of tone; and if it is extended to double its length,
triple measure ensues: —

$$\frac{3}{4} \quad \overset{\smile}{} \ \Big| \ \overset{-}{}$$

In our mode of notation the second (answering,
accented) beat is distinguished by the bar-stroke; according to the usual method of counting the beats of a
measure, the accented beat is unfortunately named the
first, and this, therefore, gives rise to a misunderstanding of
the relationship of the beats to each other; we must therefore here call attention to the fact that the second (unaccented) beat is upbeat to the following accented beat
(the *so-called* "first")

Again by opposing a second (answering) accented measure, arises the *group of two measures*

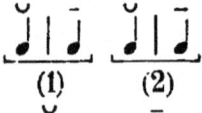

And here no practice of an opposite kind stands in the way if by 2 we now understand, in addition, an answering relationship to the 1, a heavier accent, a cadential moment; that is: *the second measure, as opposed to the first, is accented.* In like manner the first group of two measures is answered by a second, and the fourth measure, since it answers the second, has the heavier accent; the moment with strongest cadential power of the *4-measure section* is therefore the accented beat of the fourth measure

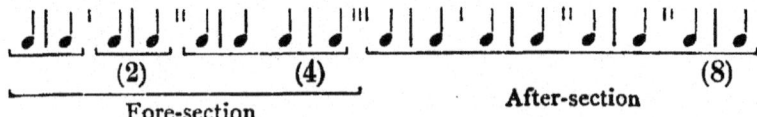

Lastly the after-section (Nachsatz) of 4 measures answers the fore-section (Vordersatz) of 4 measures: —

Pieces constructed in a strictly symmetrical manner (for instance, very many dance movements, simple songs, instrumental movements in song form) plainly follow this scheme, in that periods of 8 measures follow one another without any interruption of the symmetry.

Departures, however, from the same are very frequent, and more varied than is commonly supposed to be the case. The most important *kinds of interference with symmetrical construction,* clearly shown by the figures under the bar-stroke, are namely:

a) A marked *tarrying on the close* of certain symmetries, as in the dwelling on the accented beat to double its value (♩ | ♩): this is quite usual; and then, a conti-

iiued order of 3 measures is possible by spreading out
the accented measure to double its length

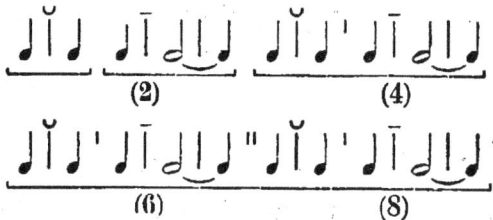

Here, from each accented measure to the next accented one there are always *three measures.* This form is
however not to be found in Bach, at least not in the Well-
tempered Clavier. But, on the other hand, in Bach and
other composers, one frequently meets with

b) the *repetition of accented (answering) form-members* (close-confirmations) which are possible in the most
varied dimensions, and, anyhow, are easy of comprehension

α) in two measure group:

also possible as 4—4a, 6—6a, 8—8a.

β) in the half-section:

(also possible as 8, 7a—8a).

γ) in the Period:

α) repeats only the accented measure of the group
of 2 measures; *β)* the accented group of the half-section;
γ) the whole of the after-section. Beethoven is fond of
employing all three kinds (in the order *γ*, *β*, *α*) at the

close of periods — first a repetition of the whole after-section, then a repetition of the last group, finally a repetition of the last measure (Bülow's "System Verkürzung" *i. e.* "System of shortening"); see for example the Sonata in D, Op. 28, first movement, the last lines before the repeat. Jóh. Brahms carries *α)* through the whole period (see the pseudo ⁷/₄ measure in the Trio Op. 101), and Bach makes free use of all these possibilities. From Tschaikowsky we learn that the repetition of the accented beat in the measure is also possible

see the composer's Op. 37 No. 1.

c) the *omission (elision) of unaccented form-members* (thus: ˉ ˇ ˉ) *i. e.* beginning greater form-members with, relatively, an accented beat, also possible in various gradations:

α) group of two measures *beginning with the accented beat of the first measure (i. e. without upbeat);* this is of usual occurrence, but mostly with the following development of the upbeat in the answering form-member. If carried right through, this form becomes a pseudo ⁸/₄ measure:

usually presented thus

as in Beethoven's "Sehnsucht":

etc.,

through the whole "Lied".

β) beginning the half-section with the accented measure
of the first group of two measures thus:

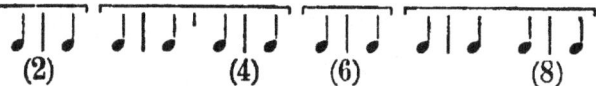

(2)   (4)   (6)   (8)

This is the most frequent form of three-measure
rhythm, also in Bach (see Well-tempered Clavier Pt. I.
fugues **1, 8, 16, 19, 20, 24,** etc.).

γ) beginning the Period with the accented group of
the fore-section (in which of course it is possible to have
also the forms c) *α* and *β*, *i. e.* beginning with the cadential
value of the fore-section — the latter being the manner
in which this formation is most frequently presented):

(4)   (8)

d) Changing the meaning of a measure from accented
to unaccented, happens, as a rule (for only thus is it easily
intelligible) when on the final note of a period another
one begins, which has previously been heard; or one with
strong contrast as regards dynamics and rhythm. Most
frequent is the change of meaning of the 8th measure to
first (this is often to be met with in pieces otherwise
normal in form), indicated by 8 = 1; but also the meaning
of the 8th measure turned back to that of 5th is by no
means rare (8 = 5), *i. e.* repetition of the after-section,
not indeed after the 8th measure, but with negation of its
cadential power; and in like manner the 8th measure
turning back to the meaning of the 7th (repetition of the
closing *group* with negation of its cadential power). A
rare case of such intricacy is the changing of the cadential value of a greater symmetry into the upbeat of a new
form-member, for example

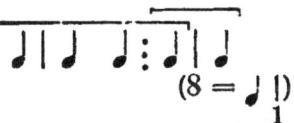

Here the accented beat with which the period concludes is changed into an unaccented beat (upbeat -— to
the first measure of a new period).

Such changes of meaning can be *prospective* as well as *retrospective*, *i. e.* they can arise as well through the compression of the beats or bars of a section, as through the repetition of the form-members; the former occurs frequently in Bach, when he makes the voices follow one another, without waiting for the last note of the fugue theme, for instance:

$$\text{(2=3)} \quad \text{(4=5)} \quad \text{(6=7)} \quad \text{(8)}$$

i. e. an 8-measure period compressed really to four measures.

Other signs employed need no explanation; the slurs are occasionally used to show more closely the construction of the periods, and the small guide indicates a division into small articulations.

Then again, the ⌢ over a note (*agogic accent*) characterises the same as the accented one of a feminine ending (with suspension).

The ♩, ♪, 𝅗𝅥, 𝅗𝅥., 𝅝. etc. enclosed in brackets at the beginning of a movement show the value of the real time-units in the above mentioned sense.

These few explanatory remarks may suffice to help the reader over the special difficulties of the author's mode of indicating harmonies, groupings of measures etc. It would indeed be unreasonable to expect the exposition of the laws by which a composer's imagination is guided to be simple, and easy of comprehension.

EINLEITUNG.

Um die Ergebnisse der vorliegenden Analysen auch für die-
jenigen nutzbar zu gestalten, welche mit den andern theoretischen
Schriften des Verfassers nicht vertraut sind, ist es notig, eine kurze
Erläuterung der zur Anwendung gekommenen neuen Harmonie-
bezeichnung, sowie auch der den Periodenbau aufdeckenden, den
Taktstrichen untergeschriebenen Zahlen vorauszuschicken.

Die neue Akkordbezifferung führt alle Harmoniebildungen
zurück auf die beiden einzigen moglichen Arten konsonanter Akkorde,
den Dur- und Mollakkord, welche beiden im Anschluss an die Auf-
stellungen der grössten Theoretiker der Vergangenheit (Zarlino,
Tartini, Moritz Hauptmann) als einander gegensätzlich vorgestellt
und bezeichnet werden, der Durakkord als die Verbindung eines
Tones mit seinen direkten Verwandten nach oben (Prime, Oberterz,
Oberquinte), der Mollakkord als Verbindung eines Tones mit seinen
direkten Verwandten nach unten (Prime, Unterterz, Unterquinte).

Die nach oben gedachten Intervalle des Durakkords werden
durch arabische, die nach unten gedachten des Mollakkords durch
römische Zahlen bezeichnet z. B.:

5 (Oberquinte)	I (Prime)
3 (Oberterz) und	III (Unterterz)
1 (Prime)	V (Unterquinte)

Der Durakkord wird abgekürzt bezeichnet durch den seiner
Prime entsprechenden Klangbuchstaben (c, d, e etc. oder cis, dis
oder ces, des) mit einem kleinen Kreuz +, das aber, wo Missverständ-
nisse nicht zu fürchten sind, auch weggelassen werden kann; der
Mollakkord wird ebenso durch den seiner Prime entsprechenden
Klangbuchstaben aber mit einer Null (o) anstatt des + bezeichnet.

Das + ist also eigentlich Abkürzung für $\frac{5}{3}$, die o Abkürzung für
$\frac{III}{V}$, beide sind daher überflüssig, wo Zahlen aus andern Gründen
doch notwendig werden (z. B. wenn angezeigt werden soll, dass die
Terz im Bass liegt, oder wenn einer der drei Tóne des Akkords
chromatisch verändert werden soll, oder endlich, wenn zum Akkord

noch weitere, dissonante Töne verlangt werden); es ist daher z. B. $\overset{c}{3}$ ein c-Durakkord mit der Terz als Basston, g $^{\,\mathrm{I}\succ}$ ein c-Mollakkord (g Unterklang kurz: „Unter g“) mit erniedrigter Prime. Die beiden Zeichen ≺ (erhöhend um einen halben Ton) und ≻ (erniedrigend um einen halben Ton) bilden die nächste Ergänzung dieser Bezifferung. Die Zahlen 2, 4, 6, 7, 8 und 9 (bezw. II, IV, VI, VII, VIII und IX) kommen ganz in der Weise der Generalbassbezifferung für die Intervalle Sekunde, Quarte, Sext, Septime, Oktave, None zur Anwendung, aber stets gedacht von der Prime eines durch Klangbuchstaben erlangten Dur- bezw. Mollakkordes aus, daher stets mit einer von der Vorzeichnung unabhängigen Grössenbedeutung; wie nämlich 1 (I) stets die unveränderte Prime, 3 (III) die (grosse) Terz, 5 (V) die reine Quinte des Akkordes ist, so bedeutet:

$$\begin{aligned}
&2 \;(\mathrm{II}) && \text{die grosse Sekunde} \\
&4 \;(\mathrm{IV}) && \text{die reine Quarte} \\
&6 \;(\mathrm{VI}) && \text{die grosse Sexte} \\
&7 \;(\mathrm{VII}) && \text{die kleine (!) Septime} \\
\left\{\begin{aligned} &8 \;(\mathrm{VIII}) && \text{die reine Oktave} = 1 \;(\mathrm{I}) \\ &9 \;(\mathrm{IX}) && \text{die grosse None} = 2 \;(\mathrm{II}) \\ &10 \;(\mathrm{X}) && \text{die grosse Dezime} = 3 \;(\mathrm{III}) \end{aligned}\right\}
\end{aligned}$$

In wenigen Ausnahmefällen kommen Zahlen vor in Verbindung mit dem gegenteiligen Klangzeichen (+, o) vor; dann bestimmt das Klangzeichen den Akkord und die Zahl einen in gegenteiligem Sinne vorgestellten Ton, z. B. o a $^{2\succ}$ = d Mollakkord (Mollakkord unter a, kurz: „Unter a“) mit Vorhalt der kleinen Obersekunde vor der Prime, also d f [a] b (= Akkord der neapolitanischen Sexte); auch die Verbindung von zweierlei Zahlen kommt vor z. B. $\overset{e^{7}\;\,{}^{0}e}{v\quad v}$ = Fortschreitung des Dominantseptimenakkords e ^{7} zur Tonika

^{0}e über bereits anticipiertem Grundtone der Tonika; der Bogen von einem Basstone zum andern ist das bequeme Mittel der Orgelpunktbezifferung z. B. $\overset{6}{\underset{1}{g\,4}}$ f g ^{7} c d ^{7} $\underset{1}{g^{7}}$ c $^{+}$. Durchstreichen

einer Zahl bedeutet die Auslassung des Tones; soll die Prime ausgelassen werden, so wird der Klangbuchstabe durchstrichen z. B f $\overset{6}{\underset{3}{}}$ = f a [c] d, g ^{7} = [g] h d f.

Zwei Punkte (• •) zeigen die Wiederholung der vorausgehenden Harmonie an.

Ein Beispiel zeige alle angewandten Mittel nebeneinander; es sei diese mit Generalbassbezifferung verlangte Harmoniefolge:

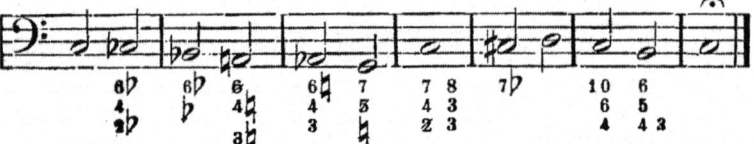

Die von Gottfried Weber (1824) angebahnte, von Fr. Schneider,
E. Fr. Richter u. a angenommene Bezeichnung der Harmonien als
Dreiklänge, Septimenakkorde etc. der Stufen der Skala kann mit
diesem Beispiele schwer zurecht kommen:

$$\text{C:} \mathrm{I}\, \flat\mathrm{II}^{7} \,\Big|\, \mathrm{I}\, \sharp\mathrm{V}^{7} \,\Big|\, \mathrm{II}^{07}\mathrm{V}^{+7} \,\Big|\, {}^{?}\mathrm{I} \,\Big|\, \sharp\mathrm{I}^{070} \,\Big|\, \mathrm{V}^{7} \,\Big|\, \mathrm{I}$$

$$\text{Ges:}\mathrm{V}^{7} \qquad \text{g:}\mathrm{V}^{7} \quad \mathrm{V}^{07} \qquad \text{d:}\sharp\mathrm{VII}^{070}\,\mathrm{I} \quad \sharp\mathrm{III}^{07}$$

$$\text{G:} \mathrm{VII}^{07}\,{}^{?}\mathrm{I}^{7}$$

In der neuen Bezifferung sieht es, unter teilweiser Mitandeutung
der Bassführung so aus:

$$c^{+}\ \underset{7}{\text{des}} \,\Big|\, \underset{3}{\text{ges}}\ \underset{5}{d^{7}} \,\Big|\, \underset{\mathrm{III}}{c^{\mathrm{VII}}}\ g^{7}_{5}{}_{<} \,\Big|\, \overset{\cdot\cdot}{\underset{\underset{1}{\mathrm{V}}}{}}\ c \,\Big|\, \sharp^{9}{}^{\flat}\ {}^{0}a \,\Big|\, d^{9}\ g^{7}_{6}{}_{\flat} \,\Big|\, c$$

Jede Chiffre enthält eine vollständige Erklärung
des Akkordes z. B. $g^{7}_{5<}\ \underset{\underset{1}{\mathrm{V}}}{\cdot\cdot}\ c$ bedeutet: der Dominantseptimen-
akkord (g^{7}) mit übermässiger Quinte ($5^{<}$) schreitet über dem anti-
cipierten Grundtone der Tonika $\left(\underset{\underset{\ }{\mathrm{V}}}{\cdot\cdot}\right)$ zu dieser selbst $\left(\underset{1}{c}\right)$ fort.

Die Grundlage der formalen Analyse bildet die Annahme der
achttaktigen Periode als eigentlicher Normalgestaltung; als
Takt (im engeren für solche Zählung massgebendem Sinne) ist da-
bei die aus zwei bezw. drei Zählzeiten mittleren Wertes (zwischen
60 und 120 M. M.) bestehende Bildung angenommen, der gegenüber
die vom Komponisten **notierten** Takte oft zu kurz (z. B. bei
$^{3}/_{4}$ Takt mit dem Tempo $\dot{\rho} = 80$), oft zu lang (zusammengesetzt,
z. B. bei $^{4}/_{4}$ Takt mit $\dot{\rho} = 90$) erscheinen.

Diese achttaktige Periode entsteht durch fortgesetzten symmetrischen Aufbau, beginnend mit der Gegenüberstellung zweier Zählzeiten, von denen die zweite der ersten antwortet und so eine erste
kleine Symmetrie (den **Takt**) abschliesst:

$$\frac{2}{4}\ \underset{1}{\overset{\smile}{\rho}} \,\Big|\, \underset{2}{\overset{-}{\rho}}$$

Diese schwere Zeit (die antwortende) ist etwas länger und wird
auch in der Regel mit verstärkter Tongebung hervorgehoben; wird
sie auf die doppelte Dauer ausgedehnt, so entsteht der dreiteilige Takt:

$$\frac{3}{4}\ \overset{\smile}{\rho} \,\Big|\, \overset{-}{\rho}$$

Unsere Notierungsweise zeichnet die zweite (antwortende schwere) Zeit durch den Taktstrich aus; unsere übliche Art des Zählens der Taktzeiten nennt leider die schwere Zeit die erste und giebt somit Anlass zu einem Missverstehen des Verhältnisses der Zeiten zu einander; wir müssen daher jetzt sagen die zweite (leichte) Zeit ist Auftakt zur folgenden schweren (ersten):

Durch Gegenüberstellung eines zweiten (antwortenden) schweren Taktes entsteht nun zunächst die **Zweitaktgruppe**:

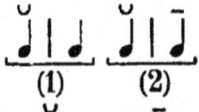

Hier steht kein gegenteiliger Usus hindernd im Wege, dass wir mit dem Begriffe der 2 die Bedeutung des Antwortverhältnisses, der grösseren Schwere, der Schlusskraft verbinden, also: **der zweite Takt ist schwer gegenüber dem ersten. Ebenso antwortet der ersten Zweitaktgruppe eine zweite, und der vierte Takt ist daher, als dem zweiten antwortend, schwerer als dieser, die schlusskräftigste Zeit des viertaktigen Halbsatzes ist daher die schwere Zeit des vierten Taktes:**

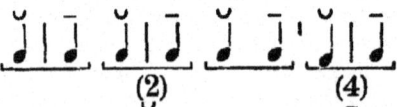

Endlich antwortet dem viertaktigen **Vordersatze** der viertaktige **Nachsatz**:

Streng symmetrisch aufgebaute Tonstücke (z. B. sehr viele Tänze, einfache Lieder, gesangsmässige Instrumentalsätze) verlaufen ganz schlicht nach diesem Schema, indem sie eine achttaktige Periode der anderen ohne Störung der Symmetrie folgen lassen.

Allein die Abweichungen vom Schema sind doch viel häufiger und viel mannigfaltiger als man gemeinhin annimmt. Die wichtigsten Arten der Störung des symmetrischen Aufbaues, welche die Zahlen unterm Taktstrich jederzeit klarlegen, sind nämlich:

a) **Längeres Verweilen bei den Abschlüssen einzelner Symmetrien.** Wie die Dehnung der schweren Zeit aufs doppelte Mass (𝅘𝅥 | 𝅗𝅥) etwas ganz gewöhnliches ist, so ist zunächst auch eine fortgesetzte dreitaktige Ordnung möglich durch Ausdehnung des schweren Taktes auf die doppelte Dauer:

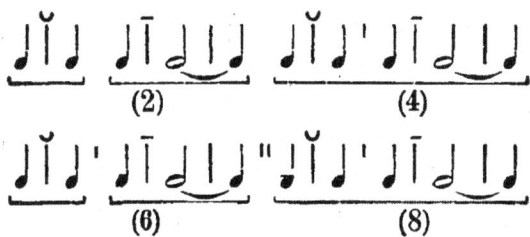

Hier sind von jedem schweren Takte zum nächsten schweren jedesmal drei Takte Abstand. Diese Form ist indes gerade bei Bach wohl nicht zu finden, wenigstens nicht im Wohltemperiertem Klavier. Häufig ist dagegen bei Bach wie bei allen Komponisten:

b) **die Wiederholung schwerer (antwortender) Formglieder (Schlussbestätigung),** welche in den verschiedensten Dimensionen möglich und jederzeit leichtverständlich ist:

α) in der Zweitaktgruppe:

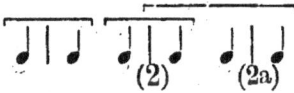

(ebenso möglich als 4—4a, 6—6a und 8—8a),

β) im Halbsatz:

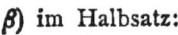

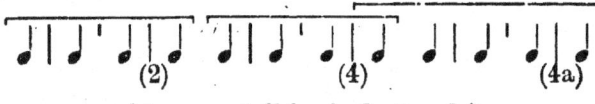

(ebenso möglich als 8, 7a—8a),

γ) in der Periode:

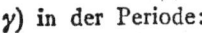

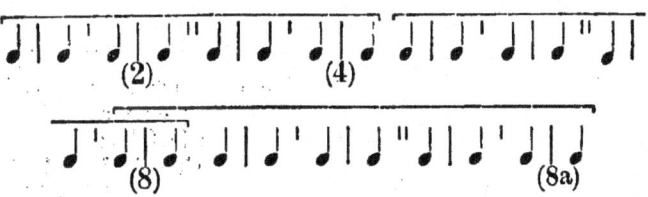

α) wiederholt nur den schweren Takte der Zweitaktgruppe, *β*) die schwere Gruppe des Halbsatzes, *γ*) den ganzen Nachsatz.

Beethoven liebt die Anwendung aller drei Arten in der Folge γ, β, α am Schluss der Periode (zuerst Wiederholung des ganzen Nachsatzes, dann Wiederholung der letzten Gruppe, endlich ein- oder mehrmalige Wiederholung des letzten Taktes (Bülows „System Verkürzung"), z. B. in Op. 28 vor der Reprise im ersten Satz; Brahms führt gern α durch die ganze Periode durch (vgl. den Pseudo $^7/_4$ Takt in dem Trio Op. 101); Bach schaltet frei mit allen diesen Möglichkeiten. Dass auch die Wiederholung der schweren Zeit im Takt möglich ist:

kann man bei Tschaikowsky lernen (Op. 37 No. 1).

c) **Die Auslassung (Elision) leichter Formglieder:** (System: Schwer — Leicht — Schwer), d. h. der Beginn grösserer Formglieder mit einer schon verhältnismässig schweren Zeit; auch hier sind mehrere Abstufungen möglich:

α) **Anfang der Zweitaktgruppe mit der schweren Zeit des ersten Taktes** (also ohne Auftakt); dieser ist etwas ganz gewöhnliches, aber meist mit folgender Entwickelung des Auftaktes für die antwortenden Formglieder. Fortgesetzt durchgeführt ergiebt diese Form einen Pseudo-$^8/_4$-Takt:

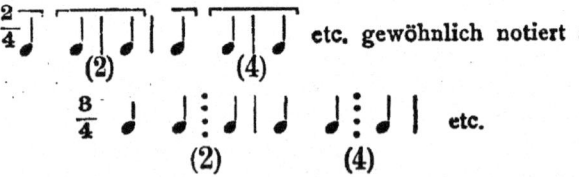

Vgl. Beethovens Lied „Sehnsucht":

β) **Anfang des Halbsatzes mit dem schweren Takte der ersten Zweitaktgruppe:**

Diese ist die häufigste Form der Dreitaktigkeit, besonders auch bei Bach, (Wohlt. Kl. Fuge I. 1, 8, 16, 19, 20, 24 etc.).

γ) Beginn der Periode mit der schweren Gruppe des Vordersatzes (wozu naturlich noch die Möglichkeiten der Mitanwendung von c) α und β kommen), d. h. schliesslich der Anfang mit dem Schlusswert des Vordersatzes — letzteres vielleicht die am häufigsten vorkommende Art dieser Bildungen:

d) Umdeutungen schwerer Zeitwerte zu leichteren, in der Regel nur vorkommend (weil nur dann leicht verständlich), wenn mit dem Abschluss eines Gedankens zugleich ein bereits dagewesener oder aber ein durch Dynamik, Rhythmik etc. hinlänglich kontrastierender einsetzt. Die häufigste Form ist die Umdeutung des achten Taktes zum ersten (diese kommt sogar in sonst ganz regelmässig sich abspielenden Stücken häufig vor), angezeigt durch (8 = 1); aber auch die Zurückdeutung des 8. Taktes zum 5. ist nicht selten (8 = 5, d. h. Wiederholung des Nachsatzes, aber nicht nach Vortrag des achten Taktes, sondern mit Vernichtung von dessen Schlusskraft), desgleichen die Rückdeutung des 8. Taktes zum 7. (Wiederholung der Schlussgruppe mit Vernichtung von deren Schlusskraft). Eine seltenere Spezialität solcher Verschränkungen ist die Umdeutung des Schlusswertes einer grösseren Symmetrie zum Auftakt eines neuen Formgliedes, z. B.:

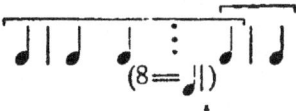

Hier wird das Viertel, welches die Periode abschliessen musste, umgedeutet zur leichten Zeit (Auftakt) des ersten Taktes einer neuen Periode.

Derartige Umdeutungen können ebensogut vorgreifen wie zurückgreifen, d. h. sie konnen ebensogut durch Zusammendrängung der Zeiten eines Satzes entstehen, wie durch Wiederholung von Formgliedern; ersteres ist bei Bach häufig, wenn er die Stimmen einander folgen lässt, ehe jede einzelne das Thema beendet hat, z. B.

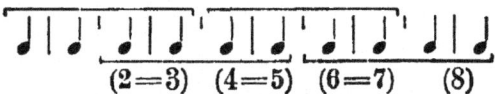

(eine achttaktige Periode auf vier wirkliche Takte zusammengedrängt.)

Die sonst zur Anwendung gekommenen Hulfszeichen bedürfen keiner Erklärung; die Bogen sind gelegentlich zur genaueren anschaulichen Abgrenzung der Phrasen benutzt und die kleinen

Lesezeichen $\left(\overline{\overline{\underline{\underline{+}}}}\right)$ deuten die Gliederung im Kleinen an.

Das ⌢ über einer Note charakterisiert dieselbe als **Schwerpunkt** einer weiblichen Endung (mit Vorhalt). Die in Klammern gegebenen

♪, ♪, ♩, ♩. ♩ etc. zeigen an, welche Werte als Zählzeiten zu empfinden sind.

Diese wenigen orientierenden Bemerkungen werden genügen, über die speziellen Schwierigkeiten der Darstellungsweise des Verfassers hinwegzuhelfen; es wäre freilich unbillig, zu verlangen, dass Darlegungen der Gesetze der künstlerischen **Schöpferthätigkeit** immer und überall wirklich einfach und leichtverständlich seien.

PRELUDE AND FUGUE IN C-MAJOR.

A prelude of truly Olympian-like repose and serenity forms the portal to Bach's majestic wonder-work of polyphonic art: the harmonies are translucent, the argument is of the simplest, the rhythm normal, while complications of any kind are almost non-existent. The motive formed by the broken chord

is carried through with iron persistency, and only in one measure is a melodic passing-note introduced:

The whole piece, concerning the allabreve-nature of which there can be no doubt (*i. e.* the ♩ are counts or beats), consists of three periods, the first and last of which, however, are extended. If we mark the melodic summits, the first (modulating to the dominant) appears thus: —

Riemann, Analysis of Bach's "Wohltemperirtes Clavier".

i. e. the cadential effect of the eighth measure is frustrated, since the under-dominant of the new key (with major seventh) enters: it therefore becomes a 6th measure (this, indeed, is a typical case), but before the period comes to an end, this 6th measure is repeated with emphasis, and with removal of the major seventh in favour of the more characteristic sixth. The second period tends back through D minor to the principal key, and dies away without disturbances of any kind.

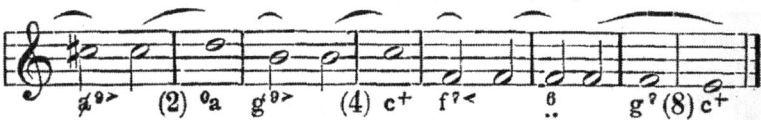

The third period is nothing more nor less than a coda, *i. e.* the piece is at an end, only the close is confirmed during 16 measures. In this closing period, therefore, we meet with all the characteristics of a coda: twice the key of the under-dominant is touched upon (at the beginning, and in the fourth measure from the end), and then there is the organ-point (pause), first on the fifth (*g*) and then on the fundamental note (*c*) of the key. It would be radically wrong (because there are 16 measures) to wish to divide the period into two; it were better to consider the fore-section repeated three times, the second and third time over *g*; and then, after a fall to *c*, comes the after-section (5th measure) during which a complete cadence is spun out.

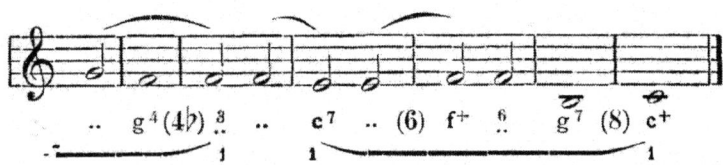

At the last measure but two, the chord-arpeggio abandons its small form, and widens out into arches filling whole bars:

The Fugue (à 4) is probably, of all the 48, the one richest in strettos, and in this respect, is a show piece of contrapuntal art. It violates scholastic rules, in as much as it does not contain *a single interlude;* but Debrois van Bruyck's depreciation of the esthetic value of this composition must be contravened: he finds in it, scholastic pedantry and monotony ("schulmeisterlicher Pedantismus und Monotonie") and calls the theme dry. First as regards the absence of episodes, the fact must not be overlooked that this piece, nevertheless, has its principal and secondary intermediate parts*). Bach, like many a later master in the department of lyrical, and less polyphonic, music (Beethoven in the Bagatelles; Schubert, Schumann, Kirchner), but also like many an old one (Couperin, Handel and Bach himself) in polyphonic dance movements, worked out with a short theme a whole — though not actually long — piece. The theme of the fugue, provided its *tempo* be not mistaken, is not in any way dry, but of a certain self-sufficient, contemplative character, and the fact that it forms a complete cadence may be the harmonic cause thereof; as it does not, however, return to the fundamental note, but in

---

*) See note next page.

1 *

its first half sinks from the fourth, in the second from the fifth, only to the third, the inner necessity of continuity is thus felt, and consequently a splitting up into too sharply defined members prevented.   With regard to its rhythmical character it must be noticed that it begins with the accented (2nd) measure (but with three graceful up-beat quavers and a feminine ending of the first motive), and has a masculine ending at the fourth measure. The contrast between the wide-interval progression in the middle of the theme and the strict diatonic steps at the beginning and end also deserves notice:

In the real, principal developments of this fugue Bach adheres throughout to three-measure rhythm — ◡ — (cf. Catechism "Kompositionslehre I p. 84 and 175), _i. e._ the other voices follow, skipping over the unaccented measure, and enter likewise on the accented one. Departure from this order becomes therefore a peculiar means of distinguishing between the intermediate, and the real, principal developments; an 8-measure period, to which only the first, but not the fifth measure, is wanting, stands out specially as episode: it occurs after the first full development. The stretto first appearing in modest form (between soprano and tenor) in this episode, as well as the cessation of the alto part, facilitates such comprehension; but after the suitability of the theme for stretto has become manifest, this special contrapuntal stimulant cannot afterwards be abandoned (for which reason in other fugues, stretto is reserved as a closing effect), and Bach now further intensifies his artifices. The fugue has not a real countersubject (principal counterpoint) appearing repeatedly in company with the theme and thereby attaining importance; the continuation of the opening alto voice when the answer is given out by the soprano:

---

*) Throughout these fugues, the "first development" in _nearly_ all cases, coincides with the Exposition.

is truly characteristic, and, with the exception of the opening motive formed by imitation from the end of the
theme, of sufficient independence to play such a *rôle*.
But from the first episode onwards, owing to the continued
strettos the possibility of turning it to such account va-
nishes; and even in the first development, to which, this
reason does not apply, Bach is content, when the theme
occurs in the tenor, to allot the opening semi-quaver
passage in inversion to the soprano, and to apportion the
syncopated "turn" motive to the alto:

He indulges in a similar (still freer) method when the
theme occurs in the bass. Also, in the further course of
the fugue, passages of a similar kind are to be met with,
but the countersubject never appears in integral form.
The theme itself, only on other degrees, plays the *rôle*
of real countersubject. The principal and most intensified
form of stretto is that of the under-fourth, likewise upper-
fifth, at the distance of a crotchet:

8va bassa.

and

Stretto also appears in the octave (at the distance of 4 or 6 quavers: see *a* II—III and III—IV), a seventh below (see *b* II—III) and a fifth below (see *b* III—IV); and finally it appears in the upper fourth at a distance of 4 quavers:

As, not only in every fugue, but in any piece of music constructed on an intelligent system, so in this fugue, three principal sections are to be distinguished: a first one establishing the principal key; a second, modulating; and a third emphasizing once again the principal key. The first section includes the 4 successive theme entries in the order: alto, soprano, tenor, bass, within the compass of two periods of the elliptical form indicated above (with elision of the 1th and 5th measures). As the theme begins and ends with tonic harmony, and does neither exceed the compass of the hexachord *c—a*, nor contain the step from tonic to dominant *(c—g)*, so the answer is a faithful transposition in the fifth. Again as the seventh does not occur, the theme can be harmonised, both in the dominant and in the principal key (in dominant, Mixolydian harmony), and thus Bach is able to introduce the Comes successively in the soprano and tenor: the soprano in the key of the dominant, and the tenor in the Mixolydian key — so that without transition, the Dux can again be brought in in the bass, and the complete exposition concluded in the key of C-major.

The little episodical period of 8 measures which joins on (stretto between soprano [Dux] and tenor [Comes] with subsequent alto entry of the Comes) modulates to the key of the dominant; it is immediately followed by a stretto completing, as it were, the former one, between bass (Dux in G) and alto (Comes on the dominant of G) with subsequent tenor entry of the Comes on the dominant of A-minor, in which key this fourth period ends with a close-confirmation of one measure. The next stretto (see above *a*) enters suddenly in the principal key: (alto Dux, tenor, bass and soprano Comes) and proceeds, by means of a deceptive cadence, to A-minor; by a rectification of three measures it is turned towards the key of D-minor with a confirmatory close of two measures. But at this moment tenor and alto enter, the former with an up-beat of three quavers, the latter with one of one quaver (stretto from the degrees *a* and *e*), introducing the theme in the dominant harmony of G, which key continues for the subsequent soprano entry of the theme on *g*; whereas at the close of the period the tenor (theme beginning on *b*) changes it to the dominant of the key of C (with $f\natural$, Mixolydian) so that the 8th measure acquires the meaning of a 4th; an appended section of 4 measures (in which occurs a triplet of counts) concludes in the principal key. The bass now remains stationary on the fundamental note of the key up to the end, while a last period (tenor and alto in stretto, see above *c*), in well-known characteristic coda fashion, introduces the natural seventh of the tonic, thus touching the under-dominant, and concluding freely in the last three measures without any indication of the theme. The middle modulating section (4 periods) is by far the greatest of the three, but by inserting a stretto in the principal key the equilibrium is not disturbed.

I. 2.

PRELUDE AND FUGUE IN C-MINOR.

This prelude is by no means a chip of the same block as the first. It is not too bold to assert that in the separate numbers of the Well-tempered Clavier Bach not only aimed at displaying technique in all positions of the keyboard, but at the same time, and once for all, in typical manner at revealing the character of each particular key. The C-minor prelude of the first part is so possessed with the spirit of the C-minor key, so full of restrained power, of passionate throbbing, that the C-minor Symphony of Beethoven and likewise his *Sonate pathétique* recur spontaneously to one's mind. And that before this remembrance Bach's work does neither pale, nor wither away and become a mummy is certainly the best proof of the mistake made by Debrois van Bruyck in speaking of "jingling and rumbling of sounds" ("rasselnde Tonrumpelei"), and in looking at it as only a brilliant note-piece, quite of an *étude* kind ("ganz etudenartig") and slightly monotonous. But it should be mentioned that Bruyck's dogmatic judgment changes later on into enthusiasm.

The construction of the piece, for the rest, is similar to that of the first prelude. It consists of three (extended) periods of which the last has decidedly a coda character (organ point on g, and finally on c, with a turning towards the under-dominant). The first period opens *ex abrupto* (6th to 8th measure) and concludes in the principal key; already at the fourth measure, the second reaches the chord of six-four, and makes a half-close on the dominant (with repetition of measures 5—8); the third period (coda) has Bach's own mark *Presto* ("rattling like hail in a storm" ["das gleich einem prasselnden Hagelwetter losbricht"], to quote van Bruyck), but in the after-section returns through *Adagio* to the *Tempo primo (allegro)*. The two-part figuration motive:

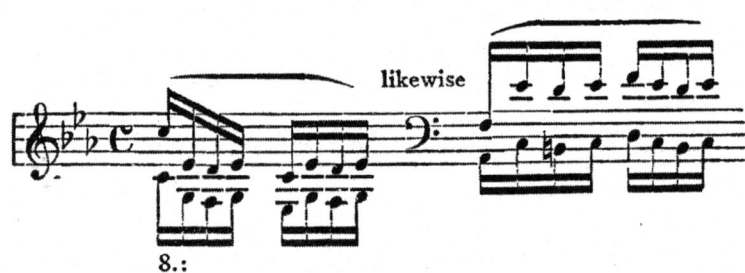

8.:

is only abandoned in the repetition of the after-section
(Nachsatz) of the second period in favour of a one-voice
motive, of wider extent, which leads to the *Presto:* —

The *Presto* itself has motives with masculine endings
($^{15}/_{16}$ up-beat)

which contrast sharply with the long endings of the first
two periods; also the two *Adagio* measures adhere to
these masculine endings, and only the final cadence restores
equilibrium by means of feminine endings prominent up
to the 10th measure of the period.

If the piece be reduced to elementary harmonic form,
noting only the melodic summits, its general construction
may easily be made intelligible:

Allegro (2 ♩) Commencement *ex abrupto* ‖ 1st period.

after-section repeated

‖ 2nd period.

‖ Presto.

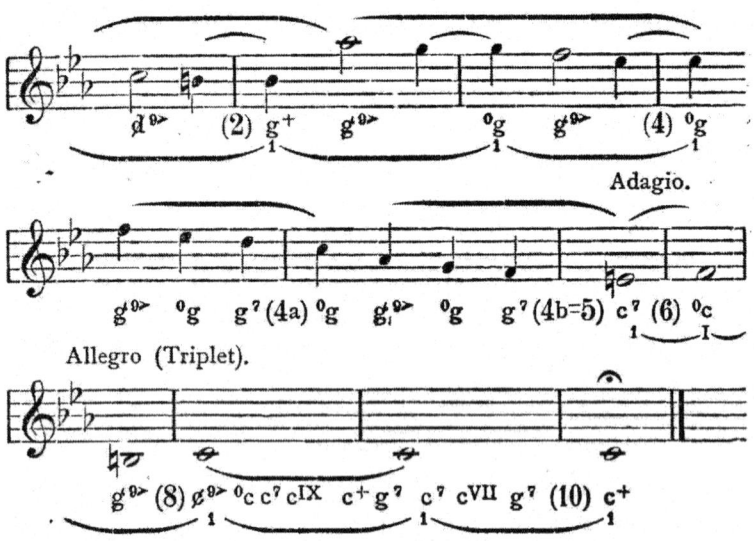

Adagio.

Allegro (Triplet).

The fugue which follows this powerful piece shows the character of the key from quite another side. The minor character, intensified by the 3 flats, naturally infuses into the mood a certain earnestness, which, however, in combination with the graceful rhythm and the somewhat obstinate repetition of the *c* in the melody, gives to the music the character of sober-mindedness rather than of energetic will. The articulation, of itself presenting an alternation between the legato of the melodic intervals and the staccato of the harmonic breaks, increases this impression of perseverance, of quiet diligence (without any haste; *Allegro quasi Allegretto*). The simple metrical nature of the theme, which occupies 4 measures without elision or insertion of any kind, is favorable to symmetrical construction of periods. Bach has therefore reserved any departures from the same ($^3/_2$ measure instead of $^4/_4$) for two of his episodes, which by that means obtain special importance and characteristic physiognomy. The theme is as follows:

The answer differs only in one note (see * in last example) from the transposition in the fifth. Though Marx (cf. Komposi-tionslehre II, Appendix J), relying on certain old editions even prefers for this note the answer in the fifth *(d)*, yet according to recent showing the authenticity of the *c* in the auto-graphs is beyond question. There remains then only to ask why Bach answered *g* by *c* and not by *d*? Although by way of proof it is sufficient to point to the old rule that the opening *step* from tonic to dominant *(c—g)* at the beginning must be answered by dominant-tonic *(g—c)*, it may be further noticed that the Dux ends in the principal key and therefore the *modulation to the key of the dominant is reserved for the Comes*, and this would not be facilitated by starting with dominant harmony. The harmony of the Comes at first is *not* that of the dominant but that of the tonic, which by addition of the natural seventh *(VII♮ = a)* becomes, without restraint, under-dominant of the minor key of the upper-dominant *(°d)*.*)

In this fugue the countersubject plays a very impor-tant *rôle*, since (supported by the principal motive of the theme) it furnishes material for a number of characteristic episodes. Comes and counterpoint follow on immediately after the last note of the theme, and bring the first period to a close: —

<hr />

*) Readers may be reminded that the *a* natural in the Comes is spoken of as natural seventh (VII♮) because it is the under-seventh from *g* (g^{VII}) thus The chord with addition of the *a* suggests the sub-dominant harmony of the key of G minor.

This countersubject never abandons the theme, and is combined with the same, whether as Dux or Comes, excepting where the theme appears as coda over the closing bass note (in the last entry but one of the theme, the countersubject is freely divided between the soprano and the middle voice).

The fugue is written *à tre*; in order therefore to make the end of the first development with the Dux in the bass the end also of a second period, Bach precedes the bass entry by an episode of four measures (in which are worked the opening motives of theme and countersubject), and thus obtains a natural return to the principal key. It should not be overlooked that the decisive close of the Comes in the key of the minor upper-dominant is a cause of the few theme entries (in all — Dux and Comes — only eight).

The (modulating) middle section of the fugue begins with an episode of four measures, in which the opening motive of the theme is thrown to and fro by the upper voices, while the bass spins out the opening motive of the countersubject into a running semiquaver passage; the period then concludes with the theme given out in the parallel key (E flat) which had been reached at the fourth measure. As at the entry of the bass, so here a second countersubject is combined with the first: it is afterwards strictly adhered to, and is, in fact, related to the first, and only appears as a third- and sixth-doubling of the same (during the first motive it is silent):

1st Cp.

2nd Cp.

A second period in the middle section, having as fore-section a free episode (in which motive *a* of the countersubject is carried on in the upper voice, and motive *b* of the same is given out in thirds by the lower voices) modulates back to the principal key, but only to introduce, in the after-section, the Comes in the alto part. Now begins the third period in G-minor, and at its close the final return to the principal key is made, in which key the concluding section remains. The fore-section of this third period of the middle section, as indeed that of the concluding section, is framed by Bach in $^3/_2$ measure (of which no heed is taken in the original notation); both are episodes **of** sequential form (evolved from the opening motives of theme and countersubject with third-doublings in the third voice), while the after-sections each show a theme entry (Dux): at the close of the middle section, in the soprano, and at that of the concluding section, in the bass. The close consists of one period, but extended, first by repetition of the second group (pause on the dominant g^7), and then by an improved cadence (the first 8th measure has the third in the bass) by means of a repetition of the closing group. It has already been mentioned that the Dux, given out once again in the soprano (with free additional voices to strengthen the harmonic effect), is appended by way of coda. Both prelude and fugue close in the major.

Observation. It is altogether impossible, because disfiguring to the fugue, any longer to read the five 3-measure groups which are real, and undeniably perceptible to the ear, as measures in groups of two (i. e. in $^4/_4$ time). The only other possible way would be to accept the order: _ ◡ _ thus

But to this it might be objected that the concluding entry of the theme would become a surplus, an extra insertion. That the sequence breaks through rhythmical order, and will well bear a *stringendo* is indeed recognized. The esthetic effect is however thoroughly satisfactory and convincing, when by the re-entry of the theme an end is put to the storm and stress of the fore-section.

I. 3.

PRELUDE AND FUGUE IN C♯-MAJOR.

Kroll has written this number in the key of D flat in place of C♯, and might plead, by way of justification that Bach, had he lived at the present day, would certainly have done the same; for, without doubt D flat is a key more familiar to us than C♯, but in his day, the reverse was the case. The C♯ prelude, however, affords convincing proof that his powers of feeling and of invention were definitely influenced by the key: this ardent midsummer mood, this flashing, glimmering and glistening ("Blitzen, Flirren und Flimmern") were evolved from the spirit of the C♯-major key; the veiled, soft key of D flat would have suggested treatment of a totally different kind. The principal thought is to be read thus: —

i. e. beginning with the accented measure, and having a long feminine ending; in spite then of the quivering figuration

it has a quiet, almost languishing character, and seems to suggest a siesta under the shade of leafy trees, on grass fragrant with blooming flowers, and all alive with the hum of insects. The quiet movement of the under part:

supports the melody without attracting attention to itself.
This thematic half-period is repeated four times (in C♯-major,
G♯-major; D♯-minor, A♯-minor), while each time, by a
graceful transition, the voices exchange *rôles.*

theme.

The first section comes to an end with the close in
A♯-minor (parallel key); the character of the piece,
however, suffers no pause in the movement, and the
following episode (passing through the keys A♯-minor,
E♯-minor, D♯-minor, A♯-minor, G♯-major, D♯-minor,
C♯-major, G♯-minor, F♯-major), with its constantly
whirling turn-shaped figure, and its octave leaps up and
down, resembles indeed a mad dance of gnats:

etc.

With the close of the second 8-measure period descending
by degrees (in this little episode I look upon the measure
motive as ♪ | ♩, so that the alla-breve character ceases

for the time, and gives place to a rhythm more of a dance kind) the key of the under-dominant *F♯-major* is reached, and the principal theme (again with ♩. as count, and therefore ♩. | ♩. as measure motive) is resumed, only in a lower position than the one it occupied during the first four repetitions — producing a truly refreshing effect, like that of a thick shady wood; but already in the after-section the key of *C♯-major* and the position of the opening of the piece return, bringing the second section, and with it the whole piece, to a close. All that follows is coda (two 8-measure periods with extensions and a short episode of four ♪ | ♩ measures, with two organ-points on the dominant G sharp). In place of the continual tremolo, appears a broken one

which intensifies the general character — everything is life and movement, everywhere there is blossom and radiance: the very atmosphere trembles; and yet the firm metrical design of the principal theme (the long feminine endings) displays to the end the same rapturous repose. The harmonic basis of the concluding section (giving the melodic points) is as follows: —

In the concluding measures great arpeggio forms, like deep sighs, writhe through a compass of almost three octaves.

The fugue (à 3) does not in any way appear to me (as maintained by Bruyck) of a humorous nature, but rather breathes peace and cheerful delight: it is of enchanting sound, and full of deep feeling. Bruyck in his impression of the piece was evidently influenced by Czerny's indication of *tempo* (*Allegro* ♩ = 104). The numerous feminine endings and harmonic subtleties are quite opposed to such hurrying (*Andantino piacevole* appears to me to give the right idea of the *tempo*).

The theme consists of four measures, without ellipses or extensions, and is therefore favourable to symmetrical construction; in the first half it is full of expression and submission, and has a feminine ending, but in the second it changes, so to speak, to a *parlando* style:

As it does not modulate, and concludes with the tonic, Bach begins the answer, not with the fifth of the dominant, but with the tonic. Thus the first melodic progression is altered, as the second *g♯* (ornamented with the long appoggiatura *a♮*) is regularly answered by *d♯* (with ornament *e♮*); the rest is faithfully transposed. Here it is with the first counterpoint (countersubject)

i. e. after the first d♯[7] Bach steers back by means of the g♯[7] to the principal key, and only in the second part of the theme does he effect the real modulation by giving to *c♯+* (tonic) under-dominant meaning (c♯[6]). Throughout the further course of the fugue the Dux is treated in a

2*

similar manner, for the feminine ending of the second measure is harmonised, not with the upper-, but with the under-dominant:

Special notice should be taken of the fact that Bach is almost painfully accurate in preserving the harmonic meaning of his fugue themes. The fugue under notice, with its many theme entries, affords a rich opportunity for anyone to become convinced of the truth of this statement.

After the Comes, the Dux is at once heard in the bass, and with the first countersubject is associated a second one which, with exception of two theme entries in which it is altered in favour of a more definite bass progression, is strictly carried out:

According to necessity a change is made in the ending, but the characteristic, syncopated, descending progression, on the other hand, is strictly preserved. The three obbligato voices appear in their entirety in four different positions, viz.: —

a) 2nd Counterpoint
   1st Counterpoint
   Theme.

b) 2nd Counterpoint
   Theme
   1st Counterpoint.

c) 1st Counterpoint
   Theme
   2nd Counterpoint.

d) Theme
   2nd Counterpoint
   1st Counterpoint.

The combination *a)* reappears, curiously enough, near the end (immediately before the coda), note for note as it is found in the first development; and just before that *c)* reappears, only with Comes instead of Dux. Also in the

episodes Bach makes plentiful and rich use of double
counterpoint, but heightens the effect of the transposition
of voices by clever additions and deviations (movement of
a voice by contrary motion). The motive material for the
episodes is: —

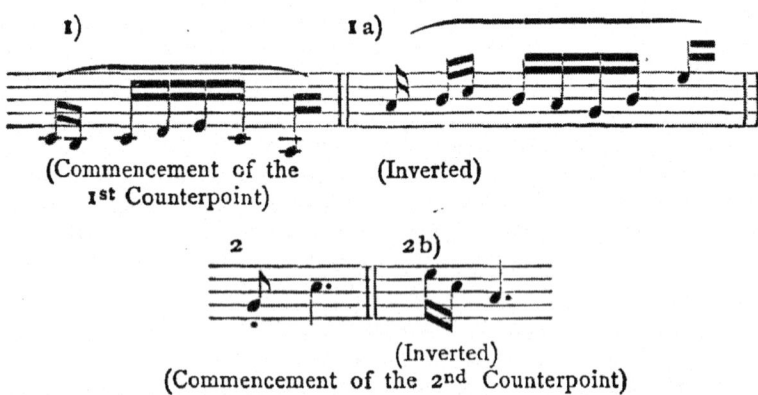

(Commencement of the   (Inverted)
  1st Counterpoint)

(Inverted)
(Commencement of the 2nd Counterpoint)

The leap upwards of a sixth taken from the commencement of the theme (which, however, soon becomes
extended into an octave leap) appears, in the third episode,
in place of the motive *2b*) in the following form

with 1) as counterpoint in the bass. With exception of
a few freer cadential formations, the above is the total
material used in the somewhat long fugue, of which we
have now to consider the general features as regards construction.

That the number of sections here exceeds three can
already be seen by the greater number of elaborate episodes,
of which no less than six can be pointed out.

The first of these appears, after the three voices have
entered regularly, and without connecting measure or measures,
as Dux (soprano) — Comes (alto) — Dux (bass). It consists
of four measures, and seems not so much fitted to lead
to a second development, as to round off the first in a
symmetrical manner (it completes the second period), and

to give to it the indispensable close in the key of the dominant. A second section now appears, beginning with a theme entry (Dux) in the key of the dominant (soprano), and ending with one in the parallel key of the dominant (alto), with an intermediate one (in the bass) in the parallel key *(A♯-minor)* of the principal key. An episode closing in *D♯-minor* completes the first entry as an 8-measure period; the second is followed by an episode of six measures (the 8th measure changing its meaning to that of 6th), and the third by an after-section with elision of the 5th measure, which strengthens the close in *E♯-minor.* The close of the second section is marked by a shake, and the crowded harmony, suggests indeed an *allargando.*

A third (most central) section — it should be noted that by the return to the principal key in the middle, a kind of rondo form is established — at first plays harmlessly with the opening portion of the theme, during which the alto accompanies with the inversion of the first figure of the countersubject (1 a); at the fourth measure the bass takes hold of the same, and now the soprano introduces the theme in the dominant (as Comes). In this case the episode leads through *D♯-minor* back to the principal key, and the entry of the theme in the soprano forms a fore-section, to which the alto at once answers (Dux in the principal key): herewith this middle section is brought to a close. A fourth section — a new episodical section — which divides the middle from the concluding portion of the fugue, just as the second divided the first from the middle portion — contains free episodical working and embraces a compass of three periods. The first of these periods brings its fore-section to a close (in which motives 1, 1 a, 2 and 2a are worked out) with the second half of the theme (the only appearance of those motives apart from the theme entries); the after-section plays again with the motives 1 and 2b, but in a somewhat long sequence, which extends its compass to eight measures (close in the principal key). The second period is firmly fixed in the principal key (the first inclines towards the under-dominant, and thus already points towards the end) and makes a half close on $g\sharp^?$. The whole of the second and third periods must be thought of as over an organ-point on $g\sharp$, which note is continually recurring; and by the very cessation of this organ-point the commencement of the concluding portion is sharply marked. Again the motive material also of the second and third periods of this long episode, consists of the commencement of the theme with a new and simple counterpoint: —

NB.

Finally the concluding portion introduces a complete development in the principal key, and this is distinguished from the one at the opening of the fugue, in that it starts at once with two voices (with theme in bass), and is completed by a postlude, not of eight measures, but of six: it is occupied with the motives 1, 2, 2a and 3, does not modulate, and, in it the bass descends to the lowest octave. But Bach cannot satisfy himself, and by way of coda makes the soprano give the Dux again twice, once quite faithfully, the second time with slight melodic alteration; in the closing motive all four voices appear in broad quaver movement.

I. 4.

PRELUDE AND FUGUE IN C♯-MINOR.

We now enter into the Holy of Holies: throughout the sum-total of musical literature there are but few pairs of pieces so full of dignity and of inspiration as these two. In the prelude the serious, sad key of *C♯-minor* expresses noble feeling, full of depth and energy. The two following groups each of two measures:

and:

(6)

the first, the commencement of the fore-section (Vordersatz), the latter, that of the after-section (Nachsatz) in the
first period, are like unto mighty gasps, or, better still, to
the yearning sighs of a great heart. The piece is built
up of five 8-measure periods (at times with considerable
extensions) consisting of developments of the same. They
are spun out in sequential form, so that the lines of the
music often become quite immeasurable, as, for instance,
in the second period

(4)

and

but in a still stronger degree in the last two periods in
which ebb and flow fill eight whole measures; the *tempo*
must not however become very slow. Czerny's Metronome
mark ♩ $=$ 92, with crotchets therefore as beats, is a
decided mistake; it corresponds with his *tempo* indication
Andante con moto instead of *Andante con espressione* or
sostenuto, if indeed *Adagio* be not the only suitable one for
it. The following may sound paradoxical, but really it is not
so: the crotchets must be taken faster than Czerny wishes,
(almost double as fast) in order to be able to follow
the ♩. as a count or beat. How would it be possible
to grasp the gigantic lines of the last period of eight
measures (before the corrected close of four measures),

if the crotchets were taken in sufficiently slow time to make ♩ ♩ | ♩ stand out as measure motive! (The 8 measures would then become 16!)

With regard to the scheme of modulation, it may be briefly remarked, that the first period closes in the (parallel) key of *E-major*, but the 8th measure acquires the new meaning of 2nd in the following period, which comes to a marked close in *G♯-minor* (minor upper-dominant). Here ends the first section. The third period passes through *B-major* (2nd measure), touching lightly on *C♯-minor* (4th measure), to *F♯-minor* (4a, in which an elision of an unaccented half measure occurs), and again settles firmly in the key of *C♯-minor*. With this the piece is really at an end, for the periods which follow, and which by their marked shortenings (elision of the 1st and 5th measures), appear, in comparison with those of the first section, highly intensified; they modulate no more, but continue to form extended close-confirmations. The harmonic scheme is as follows: —

(Deceptive cadence).

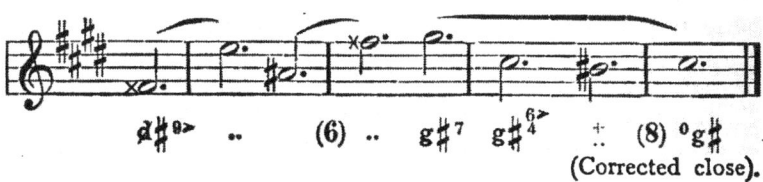

(Corrected close).

The fugue (à 5) rises like unto a majestic cathedral, increasing in intensity up to the close; and finally, where the strettos of theme and countersubject form the highest point, and, at the same time, the real close (the rest is a coda with organ-point on the dominant, and assuredly a *diminuendo* was intended), the might is simply overwhelming. The theme, evidently of allabreve character, as the merest glance will show, is one of the very shortest, and must be read:

i. e. in $^4/_2$ or indeed $^2/_1$ measure (the $\varnothing$ as count). Czerny was, therefore, utterly mistaken in making the crotchet = 112. A *tempo* must be taken which still makes it possible to trace the semibreve movement (though with a feeling of powerful restraint). As Bach repeatedly changes the closing (accented) semibreve into an unaccented one, minims, not semibreves, are, as a matter of fact, the real pulse throbs of the piece (certainly counts frequently changing meaning, *i. e.* accented becoming unaccented, would scarcely be intelligible; for, as is known, the elision of certain counts produces peculiarities of the most mischievous kind). We must therefore say that within quiet minim measure the theme nevertheless proceeds with semibreve values, and therein lies its dignity (its dignity is more than great: it is colossal). For this reason I felt compelled to mark the minim movement *Sostenuto ma non troppo*, and $\mathbb{C}$ time was changed into $^4/_2$ time, not only that the rhythmical nature of the theme might be made clear to the eye, but that one might always be fully conscious of the wonderful esthetic fact that amid plain movement in strict counts the theme pursues its superhuman course in counts of double the length.

The theme is favourable to regular construction (four full measures); but only in the third section of the fugue does Bach bring the entries so close to one another, that each set of two forms a complete period of 8 measures:

He is rather inclined frequently to bring in a new voice on the closing value (4th, likewise 8th measure), so that the fourth measure becomes fifth (the eighth, first); or we may understand it in a polyphonic sense, and look upon the closing value as such, yet, at the same time, as a new beginning; so that, the 6th measure following directly after the 4th, or a new 2nd following the 8th, the opening bar of the half section (1., 5) constantly appears not so much elided, as joined on to the concluding measure of the preceding half-section. This is something quite different from, and indeed much more complicated than the case of the unaccented opening measure of the theme, as in the first fugue, being omitted. And this is also the reason why Bach repeatedly shortens the opening note of the theme; simple elision of the unaccented measure takes the place of change of meaning; and this is not only easier to grasp, but it marks the entry of the theme in a more convenient manner.

The answer is a faithful transposition of the theme in the fifth; but it is worthy of note, that already in the first development there is an answer in the fourth (under-dominant), and, indeed (if to the four regular voices we suppose the addition of a second alto), in the first alto. This mode of answer does not, however, begin with the under-dominant, but, according to rule, with the fifth, and then proceeds to answering in the fourth; the end notes are, indeed, quite free:

The characteristic interval of the diminished fourth, extending from the sub-semitone to the third degree, has, however, been preserved. (This leads easily to the question whether, at the present day, when a knowledge of the nature of harmony and of logical tonal construction has been so powerfully developed, the fugue form actually need be limited to the reply in the fifth, or whether, as Bach has done here, a [tonal] answer on other degrees might not be attempted?)

In the further course of the fugue several other light deviations occur in the theme entries, among which the substitution of a perfect for the diminished fourth in the single major entry of the middle section (*A-major*, parallel of the under-dominant) almost explains itself; the others, without exception, concern the end of the theme, viz.: —

I, naturally, take no note of the incomplete entries in the strettos, or in the coda. Bach apparently chooses the chromatic ending at *c* with an eye to its continued development through the two alto voices.

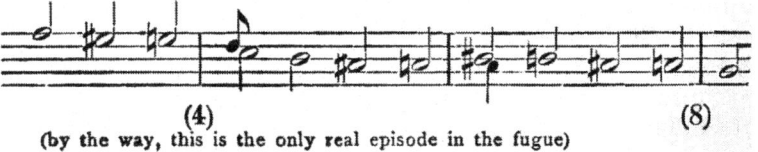

(4)   (8)

(by the way, this is the only real episode in the fugue)

Next to the real theme, which, with exception of a few connecting bars, is never absent from the plan, *two countersubjects* become of immense importance: there is first a succession of quavers of organ-like figuration, which is prudently led up to by crotchets, thus marking the beginning of the middle section,

and from thence onwards (appearing also in upward motion), it winds uninterruptedly through the voices like a garland, and only ceases at the coda. The same, although foreshadowed in the preceding second development, introduces a new, and somewhat impetuous character into the fugue, a strong contrast to the above-mentioned semibreve movement of the theme, and this character is still further intensified by addition of a formal second theme

(with occasional alteration of the cadence); it only forms a counterpoint to the second half of the theme, but is also employed in light imitation to fill up the short gaps between the theme entries. It is impossible to look upon this as a transformation of the first counterpoint to the Comes

I Cp.

on account of the totally different measure and build which it maintains throughout.

The combinations of the coda,

and

by continued imitations of the countertheme (at the distance of a minim), only once, and quite accidentally, introduce the same in a position in which the feminine ending

which constitutes the only resemblance, is presented in the same position as in the first counterpoint to the Comes.

The principal sections of the fugue are: I. *The Exposition* consisting of the first and second developments: the first concludes with a redundant entry of the Comes in the tenor in the minor key of the upper-dominant (*G♯-minor*). As Bach makes the tenor pause when the soprano enters (the five voices rise one above another, like the stories of a tower), the new entry of the tenor makes it seem as though the fifth voice was only now coming in (anyhow the five-part writing only now becomes an objective fact). The second development (beginning with 3 voices) joins on immediately: the tenor continues at once with the theme in the under-dominant, whereupon the second alto follows with *C♯-minor*, the bass with *B-major*, and the first alto with *E-major*. Both these developments occupy two eight-measure periods with the already noted elisions. II. The second section which now follows (with the running quaver passage) brings back the key of

C♯-minor (tenor) with theme entries in *G♯-minor* (Comes, 2nd alto), again *C♯-minor* (1st alto) and *F♯-minor* (soprano, for the first time with the countertheme, as conclusion of the first period of this section), once again *F♯-minor* (bass), and *A-major* (2nd alto), forming a new point of rest; but as the Dux is taken up by the 1st alto, the music continues without break. It should be noted that the appearance of the principal key at a moment in the period having such little cadential power shows a striving towards, but not a full reaching of the same; after the previous sinking down to the under-dominant and to its parallel key, that could only be accomplished by a powerful turning in the direction of the upper-dominant. Bach therefore lays hold of the dominant of the dominant ($d\sharp^7$, theme in the first alto), and returns from it to the first dominant (with the above noted chromatic progression), so that now (the 8th measure changing its meaning to that of 1st) the III. *concluding section* can open effectively, but quietly (not, as Czerny will have it, *ff* as the culminating point of the whole, but *mf*) with the entry of the Dux in the lowest position (on great C). The cadential meaning of this section reveals itself in unmistakable fashion, since soprano and tenor introduce the Dux in the principal key, and indeed with elision of the 5th and 1st measures, as at the commencement, and again (waiving the elision) the theme is given out in the under-dominant by the alto, and the Dux in still more impressive manner by the soprano, whereupon the coda, with its close strettos of theme and countertheme unfolds, the utmost fulness and power, and opens up into an organ-point on *g♯*, over which is heard once more the Dux in the soprano. But under the closing *c♯* of the soprano, the first alto gives again the answer in the under-dominant, thus forming a plagal close. It would be difficult to name anything at all comparable to the majestic rising and falling from the low bass entry at the commencement of the third section down to the very last note!

I. 5.

PRELUDE AND FUGUE IN D.

The prelude carries on ingenious sport with light motives, graceful and pleasing, rather than strong and expressive. Something resembling a spring mood pervades this piece: light-hearted beings seem to be merrily throwing flowers the one to the other. On close examination the two voices of the original notation

appear to be very delicate open work in four voices (cf. my edition):

Afterwards the music is mostly in three voices, but, from time to time, the fourth (low middle voice) again becomes perceptible, and at the commencement of the closing section the opening measures are faithfully repeated in the fifth below (under-dominant). Attention is called to the melodic progression, slightly concealed by the figuration, of the two upper voices: —

for

As the bass adheres, for the most part, to its wide steps,
it may be broken up into two voices (bass and tenor) — the
object of this remark is to enhance the merit of the piece,
which, although by no means homophonic, entirely disdains
the arts of imitation and of canon. It must be taken at
a sufficiently rapid rate for the listener not entirely to
lose consciousness of the Allabreve character established
in the opening measures.

The construction consists, indeed, principally of the
3-measure order _ ᴗ _ (*i. e.* with elision of the first and
fifth measures). The rest may be shown by setting out
the harmonic scheme, and this can be represented here
by the real bass.

(Elision of 5th measure)

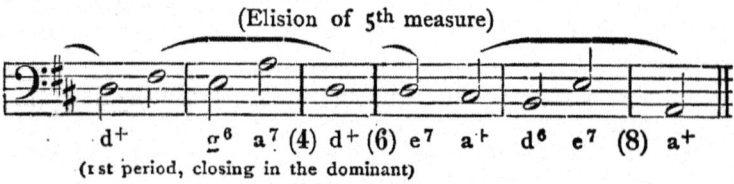

d⁺ g⁶ a⁷ (4) d⁺ (6) e⁷ a⁺ d⁶ e⁷ (8) a⁺
(1st period, closing in the dominant)

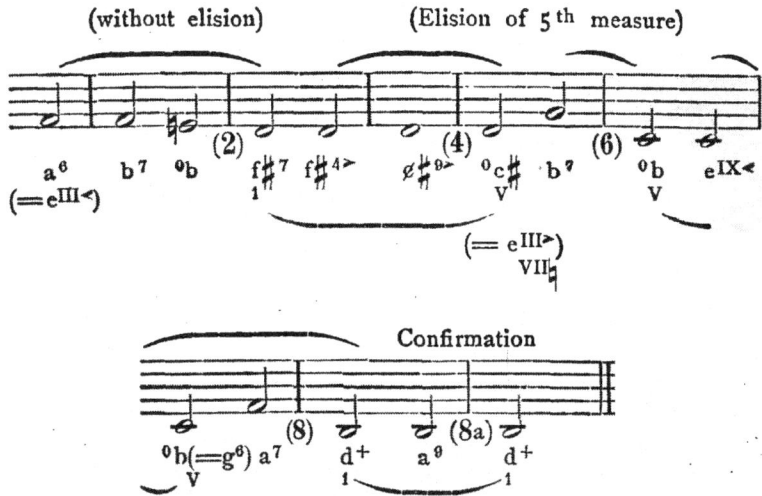

(second period returning to, and closing in the principal key; the delicate employment of the Doric sixth *a* 6 *and* 0 *c*♯ as e $\frac{\text{III}^<}{\text{VII}}$♯ should be noticed).

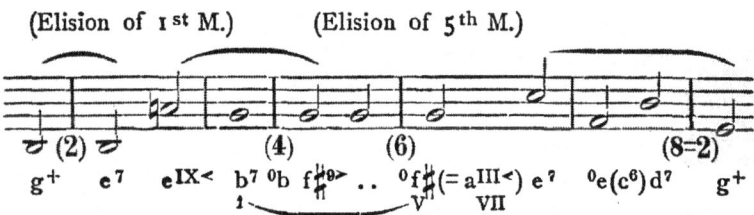

(Third period passing through A-minor and closing in G-major; real episode preparing the return of the opening principal period which springs from it by change of meaning of 8th measure to that of 2nd, but struggles upward from the under-dominant to the tonic).

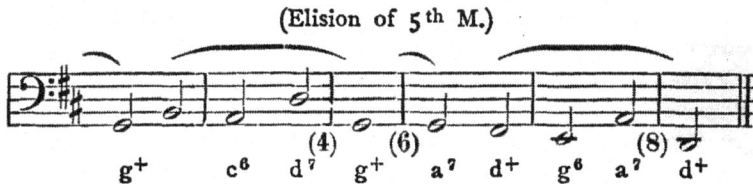

The rest is coda: there is no elision of the first measure, and at the second the dominant is grasped, and held as organ-point in the bass up to the sixth measure; there is, however, elision of the fifth, and the sixth and seventh are spread out into $^3/_2$ measure (triplet of minims). At the eighth measure the cadence is frustrated by substitution of the second upper-dominant for the tonic, so that an additional close of two measures (set out quite in organ fashion) becomes necessary by way of correction.

It is also better to interpret these closing measures as one of $^3/_2$ and one of $^4/_4$ (in notes double the length of those indicated by Bach).

The Fugue (à 4) is a powerful, proud piece which, owing to the energetic demisemiquaver run of the theme, and the consistent and persistent dotting of the quaver (♪ | ♪.) assumes a special grandeur of its own, but which, transfigured by the bright open key of *D*, only presents as it were, the appearance of, some resolute, formal nature. The movement appears almost homophonic because two or three voices move almost continually in dotted rhythm in chord fashion with only the $^8/_{32}$ run, after the manner of a Schleifer of the commencement of the theme, and a quiet semiquaver figure (derived from the free measure between the second and the third entry of the theme) by way of contrast. There is no regular first countersubject (counterpoint), for during the first appearance of the Comes the first voice merely imitates the concluding motive of the theme, and then forms a cadence in bass fashion. The answer itself is a faithful transposition in the fifth, as the theme only runs smoothly through the hexachord from the fundamental note to the sixth.

3⁕

The free double measure which joins on is as follows: —

The syncopated motive is now at once taken up by
the tenor as counterpoint to the theme entry in the alto

(while the Schleifer falls to one of the other voices, and
the "turn" ending almost entirely disappears); and in this
form has the importance of a real countersubject, which

returns for the greater number of the theme entries. We
have thus the rare case of a countersubject appearing first,
independently (in an episode), and only then in combination with the theme. The episodes which occur afterwards consist, for the most part, of the commencement of
the theme alternately with the quiet semiquaver motive,
the soothing effect of the latter being increased by its
threefold repetition in descending form.

. Now to the construction generally! Two theme entries
(bass, tenor) fill up the first fore-section; a free double
measure (see above) and the alto entry bring the period
to a conclusion in the tonic (D). Hence a second period
begins with the entry of the fourth voice (soprano), and
the fore-section of the same concludes in a free manner,
while the after-section includes a new bass entry (Dux)
— an octave lower than the first — and a new soprano
entry (with a close in the parallel key of *B-minor*).
It would be an altogether perverted method of reasoning
to speak, up to now, of a first and second development.
It would be an equal perversion to include the entry of
the fourth voice in the first development, although by
so doing the usual close in the dominant would be arrived
at. The clear, simple construction of this fugue leaves no
doubt whatever that Bach did not consider himself bound
to bring in all four voices during a first (even though
extended) period, or even during two periods, *i. e.* to complete an important form-member by the carrying out
of the theme through all four voices. As the first two
voice entries undeniably bring the fore-section to a close
in the dominant, the conclusion of the whole period in
the dominant would be decidedly tautological; Bach was
evidently, consciously or unconsciously influenced by this,
and inserted an episode before the third voice entry. He
certainly could have obtained a similar result by giving (as he

has done elsewhere) the Comes instead of the Dux to the third voice — but probably this usual way of getting over the difficulty would have incurred the danger of monotony. So now the soprano voice, hitherto absent, appears triumphantly at the opening of the second period, and indeed with the Comes, and keeps in view, quietly, though resolutely sinking downwards, until the moment comes when it can conclude with the theme in the parallel key. The second (middle) section of the fugue forms a period of considerable extent, the fore-section (M. 1—4) of which is a free episode turning towards the under-dominant; the after-section introduces Dux (alto) and Comes (tenor) in the under-dominant so that it would lead back to the principal key, but for the bass which has the deceptive cadence *a—b* in place of *a—d*. Hence the repetition of the after-section becomes necessary: it begins likewise in the under-dominant with Comes in soprano and Dux in tenor, but with a leaning towards the key of *E-minor* (parallel of the under-dominant) in which follow a low bass entry of the theme and a supplemental close. The free runs in the bass taken from the commencement of the theme give a stretto appearance to the whole of this middle section. The rest of the fugue (two 8-measure periods, the first of which repeats the after-section) stands in the principal key: it does not contain one single complete theme entry, but plays freely with the motives hitherto indicated: there are repeated cadences in D-major, but with the cadential effect easily avoided, until all four voices, note against note in full chords stringently execute the final close. Summary: first section — two periods, exposition with a turning towards the dominant; second section — an (extended) period in the under-dominant (second development); third section — two periods in the principal key (free close).

I. 6.

PRELUDE AND FUGUE IN D-MINOR.

The prelude is a pensive piece full of nobility and refined feeling, and of a certain bustling activity; with zeal, and not without a certain humour, does the bass part visit the heights and depths of its domain, feeling its way now by steps of a fifth or of a fourth, now rising or falling in long lines and by conjunct movement. The figurated upper voice must be divided throughout, as at the commencement (with up-beat and feminine ending), into members both of a higher and lower order

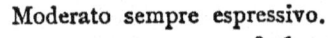

We have at first an opening *ex abrupto* (measures 6—8) on a stationary bass (organ-point), or (and after all the result is the same) a short independent little phrase of two measures ending with a full close (8th measure). The first really developed period of 8 measures which joins on to it modulates to the parallel key (*F-major*); the second soars upward to the minor upper-dominant (*A-minor*) from whence the third finds its way homeward to *D-minor*, but makes a deceptive cadence to the key of *B♭*, and on that account repeats in a more emphatic manner the closing group (measures 7—8), leading to an extensive coda by substituting *d⁷* (dominant of *G-minor*) for the concluding *D-minor* chord. This coda consists first of an organ-point on *d*, yet insisting continually on the dominant meaning of *d⁺—i. e.* it bears the impress of the key of the under-dominant (*G-minor*). But finally the second upper-dominant (♯°ᵇ) is touched upon, and a fairly long organ-point leads quickly to the end. At the beginning of the coda the semiquaver figuration partly loses its feminine ending and the lines of progression become of greater extent.

It may be mentioned that three harmonies suffice to explain the orthography of the concluding measures with their chromatic progression of diminished triads: —

(The 2nd upper-dominant = the chromatically changed under-dominant $\left[d \underset{V\!\!<}{\overset{VII}{III\!\!<}} \right]$; the 3rd upper-dominant = chromatically changed tonic [d⁊<]).

The fugue (à 3) is full of ingenious devices, for it contains not only strettos, but inversion of the theme. The latter has the two-fold formation so frequently to be met with in Bach, in its first half it advances quietly by diatonic steps, and in its second becomes somewhat passionate, concluding on the fifth and, by way of interrogation, with a shake

The uniformly ascending melody *d e f g a*, on which this thought is based, is faithfully preserved in the Comes, the latter being only the transposition of the Dux into the minor key of the upper-dominant.

This however, notwithstanding the limitation of the theme to the triad position with upper sixth and sub-semitone

$$c\sharp \mid d \ e \ f \ g \ a \mid b\flat$$

is by no means self-evident. Bach might indeed just as well have answered the progression, which taken *en bloc* = Tonic - Dominant, by Dominant - Tonic, somewhat as follows: —

or

or, indeed, like the soprano in measures 8—9 (with Neapolitan sixth *e♭*).

Over against these various possibilities the faithful transposition seems the simplest way out; the imitation of the half close, anyhow, brings the end of the Comes in the second upper-dominant, but, as Bach introduces the *E-minor* chord $\left(= d\ \overset{\text{VII}}{\text{III}}\prec\right)$ in place of the expected *E-major* chord, this acquires the meaning of the chord of the Doric sixth of *D-minor*. The theme indeed appears afterwards with deviations of various kinds, viz.: —

(Comes, M. 13 and 21.)   (Comes, M. 17.)

Comes, M. 34.)

(Comes, M. 18.)

All this shows that Bach did not look upon the harmony of the first member of the theme simply as tonic (^{0}a), but as Under-dominant — Tonic (d^{VII} — ^{0}a), so that not *d—a*, but *e—f* and *bb—g—a* had to be imitated; and this, with exception of an irregular formation (measures 8—9), is carried out in the fullest manner. Also this harmonic conception is preserved throughout in the inversions of the theme.

(Comes inversus. M. 14).

(^{0}a   a$^+$ d^7 ^{0}d)

(Dux inversus M. 28.)

(a⁷   ⁰a   a⁷   ⁰a)

Besides these two complete forms of inversion there are a great number of incomplete ones, among which, one in the under-dominant (M. 26.) After the real exposition the theme itself (in direct or inverted form), partly in real stretto, partly in easy imitation, forms the counterpoint; but, at the same time, the counterpoint (countersubject) which first accompanies the Comes, plays an important *rôle*: it is, in fact, rich in material.

a   b   c

The motives *a* and *c*, especially, are repeatedly spun out into passages; also the syncopated portion *b* often becomes prominent. Attention is specially drawn to the passage which, if not properly phrased, sounds really ugly:

It is one of the finest results of phrase indications that such old established ugly effects disappear, leaving no trace, and are replaced by others of pathetic character.

The principal sections of the fugue under notice are: —

I. *Exposition, i. e.* setting out of the theme and answer with the principal counterpoint, and establishment of the principal key: an 8-measure period with emphatic repetition of the 4th measure (change of meaning from ⁰*b* to that of the chord of the Doric sixth and full close in *D-minor*);

by a redundant entry of the theme (soprano) the after-
section appears to be in four voices. A second full close
in the tonic is set off by a Neapolitan 6th (the contrast
of this *E♭-major* chord to the *E-minor* chord in the first
full close should be noticed!), and further by the change
of meaning of the 8th measure to that of 1st in the episode
of four measures in which the concluding measure of the
theme and its counterpoint are imitated; and with a half close
on *a⁷*, the inversion of the theme is modestly announced
in the alto.

II. After four measures of transition comes the modulating second section (middle section), in which occurs,
first in the fore-section, a stretto of the Comes (on *a⁷*)
in direct and in contrary motion between soprano and alto,
with free counterpoint in the bass, and in the after-section
a stretto (firmly establishing the key of *A-minor*) in direct
motion between bass and alto (Comes or Dux? commencing on *a*). The second half of the middle section which
immediately joins on re-establishes in decided manner the
key of *D-minor*, and first of all by reproduction of the previously indicated stretto with change of voices (bass and
soprano); in the after-section there is the inversion in the
under-dominant in the alto (from *d*) imitated in the bass
(from *g*), whereupon the soprano brings the period to a
close with the complete inversion of the Dux. But towards
the close the alto enters with the original Dux, and the
bass attempts a stretto with inversion of the same; but
by this the 8th measure becomes the 1st of the closing section.

III. The concluding section (coda), for the rest, is of
free form, and turns, by way of preparation for the end, to
the under-dominant (*G-minor*), but at the 4th, and again at
the 8th measure makes a full close in *D-minor*; the after-
section is increased in intensity (in measures 5—6 Comes
on *d⁷*, *i. e.* the key of the under-dominant once again) by
means of a triplet of measures before the close (in place
of measures 7—8), which owing to sequence formation is
easily perceived, and would well bear *stringendo*. Finally,
a close confirmation of four measures introduces once more
a stretto of the Dux on *d⁷* in bass and alto; and appended
to it is still a close-confirmation of one measure in six
voices: here the opening motive of the theme forms a
counterpoint to its inversion, and both are strengthened
by thirds (major close):

I. 7.

PRELUDE AND FUGUE IN E-FLAT.

Strange that, as yet, no one has noticed that the grand piece with strict writing in four voices which figures as prelude, is itself a powerful fugue worthy to be placed by the side of the fugues in *C♯-minor*, *E♭-minor* and *B♭-minor*. Who knows whether some passing whim may not have induced Bach to follow the piece by a second fugue of totally different character. A close examination shows — as indeed Bruyck recognized — a binary, likewise ternary division of the "Prelude", as I have clearly shown in my edition by different *tempo* superscriptions (*Allegro deciso* — *Poco Andante* — *Tempo I^{mo}*). In my opinion the first two sections compose the real prelude (with half close on the dominant), while the third (three times as long as the other two together) is a fugue of considerable development, in reality a double fugue. But again there is a striking relationship between the thematic material of the preluding portion and of this fugue; and this may be seen first in the quiet second section, of which the following is the motive:

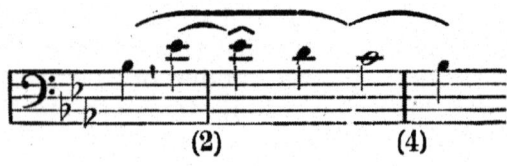

(2)　　　　　　　(4)

while the theme of the fugue appears thus:

The first section proceeding in energetic semiquaver movement with the figuration motive

embraces, finally, the very same progression of fourths (likewise fifths) and has similar syncopated feminine endings; the opening may be reduced to crotchet movement somewhat thus: —

The key of the dominant ($B\flat$) is reached at the 8th measure of the first section; the bass remains stationary on $b\flat$, and the upper voice blusters first down, and then up again, in increased movement (demisemiquavers), accentuating, by means of a shake on the fourth ($e\flat$), a close confirmed by two measures.

The tenor enters on the concluding note with the above-mentioned motive, which now appears in stretto form in the four voices: —

The notation in ³/₂ time which I have adopted, does not show the rhythmical plan in an altogether clear manner, but it may perhaps be preferred to the more correct

with its many changes of meaning; besides, the absence of figuration of any kind would easily lead one to regard the minims as the beats or counts. This section anticipates as it were, the strettos of the fugue theme, or — if one will — causes the full, definite theme to be evolved from the motion and fermentation of the closest imitations; the beginning of the real fugue therefore, like that of the ³/₂ middle section, is prepared

The countersubject appears then simultaneously with the theme, and is afterwards adhered to so strictly, that one can scarcely refrain from naming the piece a *double fugue.* Its first half is evidently evolved from the figuration motive of the introduction, but as the striking upwards towards the seventh is replaced by progression downward of a second and long feminine ending, it appears formed in quite an independent manner; on close examination the second half reveals itself as a direct imitation of the first theme member:

The answering of the theme differs from the usual plan in as much as the progression fifth—prime is not responded to by prime—fifth, but (strictly) by prime-fourth:

The Comes then, from first note to last, is a fourth
higher than the Dux, and this was absolutely necessary
inasmuch as the Dux enters in the dominant key (har-
mony of the Dux: $b\flat^{+}$ — $e\flat^{6}$ — f^{7} etc; of the Comes
$e\flat^{+}$ — $a\flat^{6}$ — b^{7} etc.), *i. e.* the Comes adopts the under-
dominant as counterweight, but only its harmony, not its
key (cf. *c*). This strict answering in the fourth is undeniably the reason why the fugue has not been recognized
as such; and the fact that theme and countersubject appear
simultaneously, renders recognition still more difficult.

The order of entry in the exposition is

Soprano: . .   . . . Countersubject
Alto: Countersubject Theme
Tenor: is as yet silent . . . . . .
Bass: Theme —   free

As however the second half of the countersubject
imitates, as a matter of fact, the first half of the theme (in
the octave), the principal motive appears to run through
the four voices

(Bass)   (Alto)

(Alto)   (Soprano)

i. e. the first development comes to an end. After an insertion
of two measures leading back to the dominant, the second
joins on, with the Dux introduced by the tenor which
hitherto has been silent, and with the countersubject in
the bass (the first notes of which, owing to the conduct
of the bass part, are wanting). As this tenor entry is
really the first appearance of the fourth voice (the second

voice entry of the first development must be understood
thus: —

i. e. the first *e♭* of the alto is really an octave too high, but
as the bass takes the low e♭ required, this is not noticed)
it might be reckoned as part of the exposition; anyhow
it is better to acknowledge the apparent existence of a
fifth voice rather than to look upon it as an incomplete
second development. The first section of the fugue extends then over the next interlude (in which the opening motive of the countersubject is used), unto the close in *G-minor*
(parallel of the dominant), *i. e.* up to the commencement
of the middle section with widely developed modulation
and numerous strettos, which extends up to the last
bass entry of the theme (after the long pause in the
bass voice). The strettos answer generally, to those of the
*Andante-*episode mentioned above, but introduce the theme
in its new form, around which plays, for the most part,
the opening motive of the countersubject (the principal
motive figuration of the whole piece):

With above third stretto, the first sub-section of the middle part of the fugue (with lively modulations — G-*minor* — F-*minor* — C-*minor*) may be considered at an end: the second, and so to speak, the heart of the middle section, is again simple in form: there is an absence of stretto (instead of which the theme is again combined with the complete countersubject), and a return is made to the principal key; the entries (after a not very strict one [*f b♭ g c d b♭*] in the bass) leading back to the principal key are:

```
Alto: Countersubject . . . . . . . . . . . .
Tenor: Comes          . . . . Countersubject
        Bass· Dux . . . . . . . . .
```

after which free modulation again takes the upper hand (theme starting with *c—f* in the tenor, and with countersubject divided between the alto, soprano and bass; then theme commencing *d—g* in the alto, around which plays the opening motive of the countersubject), whereupon the theme is once again given out by the alto, but opening with *a♭—d♭*, while soprano, tenor and bass again divide among themselves the countersubject. The modulation section concludes with the Comes given out by soprano (*e♭—a♭—g—c—b♭*) with the countersubject in the alto, after the concluding member of which, however, follows on the whole Comes, while here countersubject is in the soprano. From this small entanglement the Dux — commencing the concluding section — emerges in the bass, followed by the theme (*c—f*) in the alto, the Dux in the soprano (with *g♭* in place of *g*, organ-point on the dominant), and finally by the Comes in the alto (organ-point on the tonic); and thus follows a last complete development.

In contradistinction to the seriousness and strength of this powerful piece, the *second* fugue (à 3), a superfluous addition, seems almost like a harmless merry postlude. Who will venture to say whether the central motive of the theme with its tone succession *e♭ | a♭ g a♭ c b♭*, recalling the theme of the great fugue, was the result of chance, or of intention, or the unconscious assimilation of creative genius? The theme (which must not be taken in hurried tempo) is as follows:

4*

The answer varies considerably from the simple transposition in the fifth, first in that it substitutes for the ambitus of the opening motive Fifth — Prime, the Octave — Fifth ($b\flat$—$e\flat$, $e\flat$—$b\flat$) smaller by one degree; but as the second half of the theme makes a full close in the dominant (f^2—$b\flat^+$), the unavoidable task of reestablishing the principal key falls to the Comes, and this can only be achieved by an answer of this second half in the fourth:

The arpeggio motive which leads to the counterpoint here indicated subsequently disappears only during the various theme entries, but forms the chief material of all the episodes. The first, which is inserted between the second and third voice entries, and forms the fore-section of the second 8-measure period, opposes to this motive an expressive, syncopated one, of which also much use is made further on

(2=3)

In the second *intermezzo* entering on the dominant at the close of the exposition, bass and soprano toss to and fro the motive leading to the countersubject, while the alto, on the other hand, gives out a new chord motive in quiet quaver movement:

The structure of the fugue, for the rest, can be easily grasped: there are no strettos or other complications. The total number of theme entries is nine, of which, in addition to the first three, a single appearance of the Comes in the soprano belongs to the first (foundation-laying) section of the fugue; and only two occur in the modulating middle section (modulations to C-*minor* and G-*minor*) viz. Comes in the alto, Dux in bass: both in C-*minor*. The last three are in the principal key (Comes in the bass, Dux [only beginning in *a♭*] in the soprano, Comes in the alto as in the great first fugue, with *g♭* instead of *g*, over a repeated *b♭* after the manner of an organ-point). This small fugue is therefore a model of simplicity and naturalness — unless, indeed, one should give a false reading of the motive leading back to the principal key:

Anyone who overlooks the connection between the semiquaver following the rest in the upper voice, and the preceding motive, will not give a very smooth rendering of the passage.

I. 8.

PRELUDE AND FUGUE IN E♭-MINOR.

It was found possible to describe the character of
the *E♭-major* prelude and of its great fugue as strength
combined with seriousness and dignity — and thus answering to the general character of the key of *E♭* (though
the second fugue shows that it can also present a more
friendly aspect), but here the agreement between the general character of the key and the contents of the Bach
idea is far more imposing. The prelude, with deep, digni-
fied solemnity, advances in ³/₂ measure; the longdrawn
lines of the melody display great and noble feeling: now
clear eyes full of love seem to be gazing at us, now deep
sighs are heard, sighs of pain at the limited power
of human beings who are able to realize only a small
portion of unlimited will; so, at least, would I explain the
mighty tearing-asunder of the voices at the beginning of
the second half: —

The main features in the construction of the piece
are as follows: —

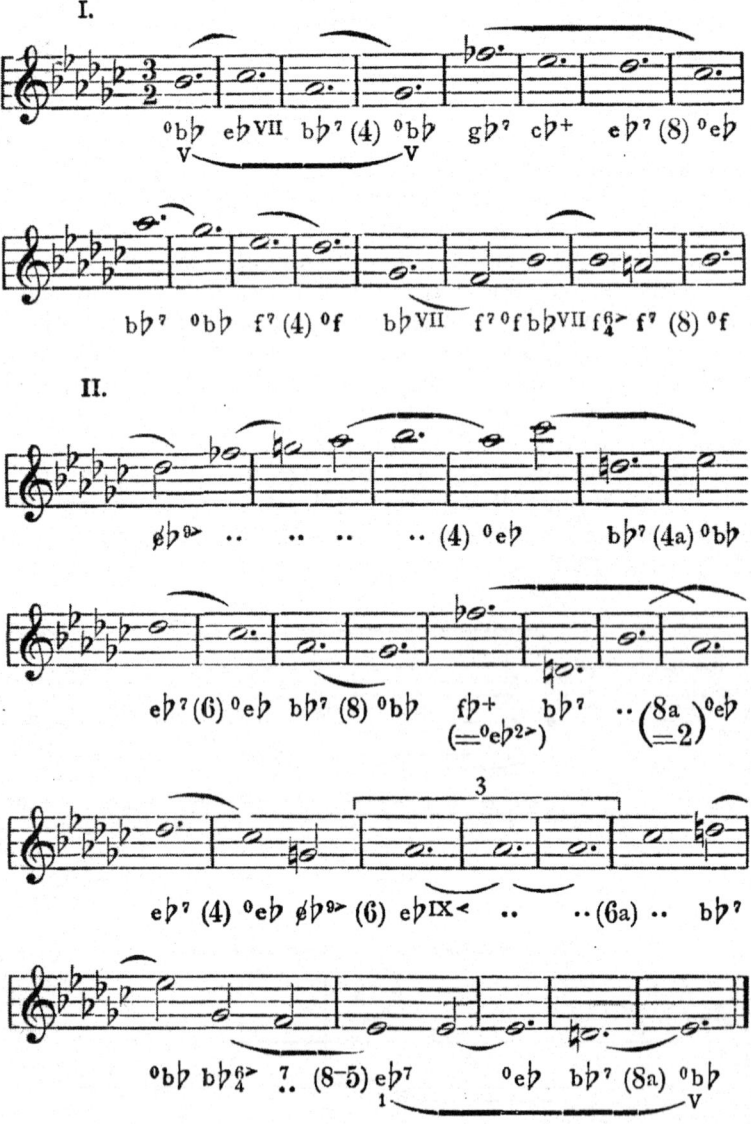

i. e. the first (smaller) half (2 periods of 8 measures) has
a cadence in E♭-*minor* with transition to the under-, and

close in the upper-dominant; the second (two periods with
extensions) has a broad chain of chords of the diminished
seventh (chords of the lowered 9th without prime, $\flat^{9}$
$\flat^{IX}$), but without real modulation; and at the chief points
of rest it makes full (likewise deceptive) cadences.

The fugue (à 3) is possessed of the same earnest mood,
but it is milder, softer, and refrains from all sharply
marked rhythm or bustling figures, pursuing its course
from beginning to end in quiet crotchet and quaver movement. If anywhere, it is indeed here that the cold
judgment of K. v. Bruyck seems out of place: I cannot imagine how anyone can speak of this noble, deeply pensive
fugue, breathing so fully the spirit of the tonality, as „made“
music. The theme was not shaped in order to allow of
many combinations; rather did the mystic character of the
key (as in the *C♯-minor, B♭-minor,* also in the *F-minor*
and *B-minor* fugues of the first book) compel the master
to display the fullest wealth of his art; and thus the workmanship became unusually profound. As a matter of fact
the *E♭-minor* fugue became, as we are about to show in
detail, a wonder-work of contrapuntal art.

The theme commences with the fundamental note,
rises to the dominant, and then sinks from the upper
second of the latter, first by degrees, down to the third,
then directly to the fundamental note; but there is another
rise, this time to the fourth, from which a descent by
degrees is made: —

Dux.

Thus we really have a two-fold close-confirmation,
first an emphatic one of one measure, which transforms
the close on the third into one on the fundamental note,
and then a broad, quiet one of two measures. As the Dux
remains firmly in the principal key, and, indeed, makes a
full close in the same, the Comes has to modulate to the
dominant; not to spring to the dominant key, but to pass to
it from the harmony of the tonic. We therefore have again
e♭ — b♭ answered by *b♭ — e♭* at the commencement of

the Comes, whereas the remainder fulfils its task by faithful transposition in the fifth:

Comes.

(8)   (8a)   (8b)

The Comes enters on the concluding note of the Dux,
changing the meaning of the close-confirmation (4b) into
that of an opening measure (6). Dux and Comes thus
form together the first period. The fugue has no real
countersubject (principal counterpoint to the theme), for
later on the theme itself (by stretto) becomes counterpoint;
still it should be noticed that quaver movement by degrees through four notes, rising or falling as at the opening
of the theme:

is specially preferred by Bach, and is extensively employed,
not only in the episodes, but in the counterpoint accompanying the entries of the theme. By that means the
quiet movement of the whole piece is essentially brought
about. We will now examine the separate sections of
the fugue.

The *Exposition* comprises, first of all, the three voice
entries — alto (Dux), soprano (Comes), and — after the
insertion of a tree half-period — bass (dux); but after
another short interlude the bass (marking, as it were, a
fourth voice) enters with the Comes (with some notes
chromatically altered), effecting a modulation to the dominant *(B♭-minor)*, passing through the parallel key *(G♭-
major)*, and forming (partly with elision of the 1st and 5th
measures) two periods. When this section has arrived at a
definite close, a *second section* (the 8th measure becoming
a 2nd) commences, a special feature of which is *stretto
of the theme in direct motion.* The three strettos are

1. Soprano: Dux (in *B♭-minor*) ⎱
   Alto: ,,   ,,   ⎰ at distance of 2 crotchets
   Bass: free counterpoint.

2. Soprano: Comes (f-$b\flat$-$c\flat$-$b\flat$ etc.)   ⎫
   Alto: „   ($b\flat$-$e\flat$-f-$e\flat$ etc.) NB. ⎬ at distance of
   Bass: „   ($g\flat$-$c\flat$-$d\flat$-$c\flat$ etc.)   ⎭   1 crotchet

3. Soprano: Comes ($e\flat$-$a\flat$-$b\flat$-$a\flat$ etc.) ⎫ at distance of
   Alto: „   ($a\flat$-$d\flat$-$e\flat$-$d\flat$ etc.) ⎭ 2 crotchets.

These lead to the remark that from the beginning of this second section the Comes abstains from the step of the third after the step of the fourth, and thus becomes more like the Dux; and from this we clearly perceive an **important law of formation in fugue,** viz., *that it is far less a principle that Dux and Comes should differ from each other than that they should resemble each other: considerations of modulation in the exposition* cause the many variations of the Comes from Dux. The composer willingly takes advantage of the free choice at his disposal between the step of fifth or that of a fourth (where such occurs) at the beginning, and this double form also plays an impoitant *rôle* throughout the present fugue. In smaller and simpler fugues it is desirable that the distinction between Dux and Comes, even in small features, should be maintained; but in more complicated fugues, on the other hand, the *unity of form of the theme* (as a collective conception for Dux and Comes) ought to be preserved, especially where (as is here the case) it passes through transformations by inversion, augmentation, etc.

A *third section* of the fugue is marked off by the entry of the *theme in inversion*, at the close of the third stretto, when the parallel key of *G♭-major* is reached. In this 3ʳᵈ section Bach carries through the *inverted theme* without further complications, *i. e.* it occurs in the soprano ($g\flat$—$d\flat$—c—$d\flat$ etc.), alto ($a\flat$—$e\flat$—d—$e\flat$ etc.), and bass ($e\flat$—$b\flat$—$g\flat$(!)—$a\flat$ ʟtc.), the two other voices joining in each time with free counterpoint. We have now returned to the principal key (further established by an interlude of 8 measures) for the purpose of beginning a new section in it.

The *fourth section* which now follows introduces first two *strettos of the inverted theme*, the first quite strict (soprano and bass, both with Dux in *E♭-minor: $b\flat$—$e\flat$— d—$e\flat$* etc.), the second freer (alto: $e\flat$— $a\flat$—g—$a\flat$, soprano: $a\flat$—$e\flat$—$d\flat$—$e\flat$ etc.), the former at a distance of two crotchets, the latter at the distance of one; then a three-fold stretto (bass, alto, soprano) of the Comes in direct motion (with *f♭* instead of *g♭*) in *E♭-minor*, at the distance of a crotchet; further, a three-fold one of the inverted Dux (bass, alto, soprano) in *G♭-major*; and finally, a perfectly plain appearance of the Dux (but with *f—b♭* instead of *e♭—b♭*!) in *E♭-minor* in the soprano, with free writing in the other voices: this simple theme entry is as a foil to set off the immense complications which now ensue!

The remainder of the fugue — now keeping closer to the principal key —, the real *concluding section*, introduces the *theme in augmentation combined with the theme in its original form, now in direct motion, now in inversion.* The three strettos thus formed are:

1. Soprano: free, then Dux (inverted)
   Alto: Dux (*f—b♭*, direct) then free
   Bass: Comes (in augmentation).
2. Soprano: free, then Comes in *C♭-major*
   Alto: Dux in *G♭-major* (*a♭—d♭* in augmentation)
   Bass: Dux in *G♭-major* (*a♭—d♭*), then free.
3. Soprano: . . . Dux in *E♭-minor* (*f—b♭*, in augmentation)
   Alto: . . . . . . Dux in *E♭-minor* (*f—b♭*) then Comes in
   E♭-minor
   Bass: Dux in *E♭-minor* (*f—b♭*), then free.

Only feel with full intensity the power of such gigantic lines, such as those of the soprano from the beginning of the last (10th) stretto up to the end, and you will marvel at the mighty grandeur of the old master:

The calming tendency of the theme, and, as it were, its philosophical superiority, appear here raised to a truly superhuman degree.

I. 9.

PRELUDE AND FUGUE IN E.

I am not certain whether writers on esthetics are really agreed that *E-major* is specially the key of deep green, of fully developed spring; it would be interesting to know the results of the late Prof. Dr. Fechner's enquiries respecting the parallelism between sensations of colour and tone. Anyhow, one has only to contrast the present number in the key of *E-major*, especially the prelude, with the preceding prelude and fugue (especially the latter) in *Eb-minor*, in order to understand that music can concern itself with deep speculation of a religious-philosophical character as well as with the lively enjoyment of nature. The light arpeggio triplets with their delicately moving summits (as though ruffled by a soft breath of air), and the cosy little shake of the feathered singers concealed beneath them, wave like branches adorned with fresh leaves: below all is peaceful (stationary bass, and slow, onward-gliding middle voice)

(2)

Though this character may apply specially to the opening half section, and to its return in the dew-fresh key of *A-major* (beyond the middle section), yet no part of the piece is in contradiction with it.

The construction with regard to metre and modulation is fairly simple. From a previously established point of stress of highest order — from the moment of rest, the starting point of fresh life — springs first a period of eight measures, with emphatic repetition of the fourth

measure (the close removed from *E-* to *B-major*), and
with intensified activity in the last group (7th to 8th measure) by means of a triplet measure; and then the close
in the dominant key is set aside by the bass (which advances to the minor third *d*), but restored by four appended
measures. A second period turns towards *F♯-minor*
(bb⁶ [=*f♯*ᵥᴵᴵ₁₁₁<] — *c♯⁷*), whereupon four intermediate measures (⁰*c♯* [=*a⁺*] — *d⁶* — *e⁷*) prepare the repetition of the
first (principal) period in the under-dominant. As this is
faithfully transposed, it leads finally to the principal
key; the first close is again set aside by the progression
of the bass to the minor third (*g*), and restored by four
appended measures; but it is once more frustrated by means
of a deceptive cadence (*b⁷* — ⁰*g♯* [= *e₆*]), and it comes finally
to an end, in plagal form, and with another triplet measure.

The very ruling tendency towards the under-dominant
(A-major and its parallel *F♯-minor*) from the moment of
entry of the second period, agrees well with the character
of calm content, delight in human existence.

In the fugue (à 3) one feels something of the joy of
a wandering life which indeed well befits the spring-mood
of the key. The energetic run of the short theme (alto),

is not peaceful enjoyment, but resolution, active energy.
The semiquaver movement of the second motive continues
without interruption until the close of the whole fugue,
and first, as countersubject (counterpoint to the Comes),

a   b

then, as filling up until the entry of the third voice (bass),

with 6th measure taken as 7th. Here the sixth parallels appear to show us two wanderers arm in arm. The syncopated motive, which is here taken up by the alto part, is likewise turned to account further on, and first in the immediate continuation:

This elevated mood becomes more intense still in the next episode (over the moving bass busy with the motive *a* of the countersubject), and in the following voice entry:

The hearts of the wanderers expand, and in jubilant tones sounds again the theme in the soprano (the Dux in a higher position). I leave to the imagination, once aroused, to complete the picture, and only point, besides, to the episode after the second development, in which the bass moves along somewhat painfully, and the alto sighs from weariness, while the soprano advances with merry hum:

In the exposition the fugue has two complete developments in the principal key with the following order of
voices: alto (Dux), soprano (Comes), bass (Dux); soprano
(Dux), alto (Comes), bass (Comes). The middle section
is limited to a modulation to *C♯-minor* (parallel), and introduces in this key two theme entries (soprano: Dux,
somewhat free; alto: likewise Dux), and includes only an
incomplete period (measures 4 — 8) and one of 8 measures, also, if one will, the four leading-back measures.
The concluding section (entirely in the principal key) has,
first of all, a complete development (bass: Dux, soprano:
Comes, alto: Dux), and after a free imitation of the great
episode of the middle part in the principal key, still an
incomplete one (soprano: Dux, alto — after an episode
of four measures — Comes). What simplicity in the dis-
position and development as compared with the gigantic
fugue in *E♭-minor!*

<hr />

I. 10.

PRELUDE AND FUGUE IN E-MINOR.

The two following pieces are specially remarkable.
The pale coloured key of *E-minor* suggested to Bach two
ideas totally differing from each other. The prelude is
full of passion, of painful palpitation, of impetuousness.
It seems as if it were a pianoforte arrangement of some
Trio for violin, lute, and harpsichord, and would best he
interpreted if read in that spirit:

Gravo, patetico.

All three instruments (let it be granted to me to work out my idea) carry out their parts in a consistent manner, until the entry of the *Presto* (indicated by Bach himself), *i. e.* somewhere about the middle of the piece. But the contents of this *Presto* only differ in appearance from those of the first section; a glance at the lower voice shows that the beginning of the same is only the transposition of the opening measures from *E-minor* to *A-minor*; but the violin has been carried away by the lively movement, and now the harpsichord follows, for the most part, in 6ths and 10ths, while the lute is silent, at any rate is no longer noticeable: —

Harmony:
(Lute)

The metrical and harmonic structure will become clear from the following: —

First Part.

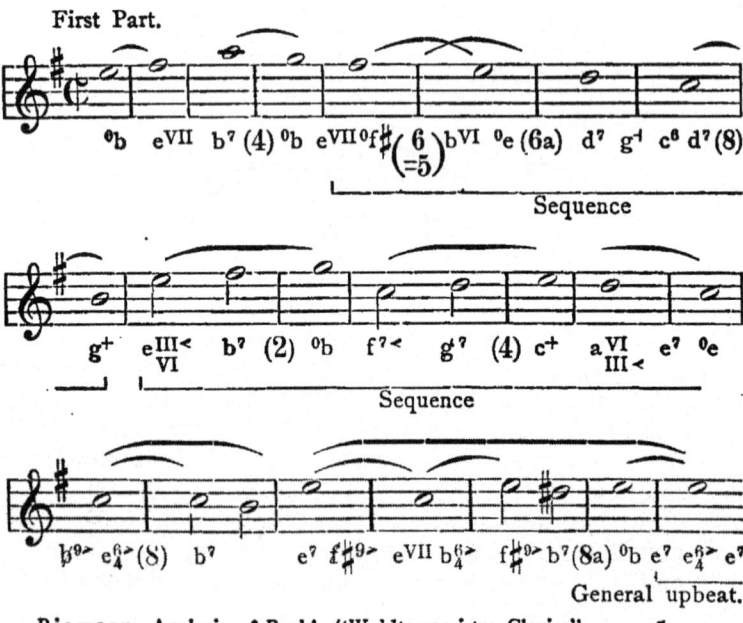

Second Part (Presto).

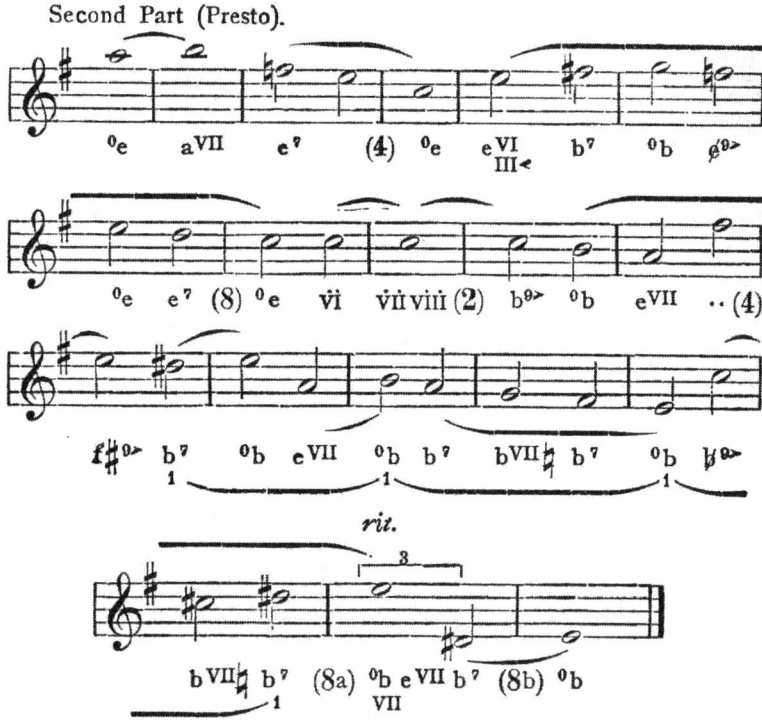

The Fugue — the only one of the Well-tempered Clavier in 2 voices — is of somewhat mournful mood, and yet there are no painful convulsions: it is rather of a contemplative character, like the beholding of nature clad in its autumn garb, when even the falling leaf and the bare-becoming branches afford esthetic enjoyment. The relationship of the theme to the *E-major* Prelude may not be a chance one; anyhow it is instructive to note the same, and, for the grasping of the meaning, important.

The theme consists, apparently of three measures, but in reality has four, since by an unexpected harmonic turn the second measure becomes third (the note b [1] on which a close is possible becomes a long appoggiatura [4]):

The actual motive (see the notes marked with upward stems), clearly perceptible through the continued semi-quaver movement, actually makes the fugue more or less in 3, instead of 2 voices (which must of course be attended to in performance). As the Comes enters on the last note of the Dux, the fourth measure really becomes fifth, so that the whole period of 8 measures appears contracted to 5 (extending to the first quaver of the fifth bar). The order of reply is, indeed, altogether irregular. For as the Dux modulates to the dominant, the Comes, according to right and custom, ought to have modulated back, some-what after this fashion:

to which, from a formal, technical standpoint, no exception could have been taken. Perhaps, however, the full, satis-factory rounding off of the period did not fit well with the composer's mood, or perhaps Bach was anxious to imitate strictly the chromatic progression — anyhow he preferred the strict order of reply in the fifth, which leads him at the end of the Comes to the dominant of the dominant $(f\sharp^{+})$:

so that the period, and with it the exposition, shows no
quiet establishment of the principal key; and only with
the parallel key at the end of the annexed episode of
six measures ($1—4$, $3a—4a$) is a point of rest reached,
which however becomes the starting point of new move‑
ment, for now commences the second development on the
concluding note (soprano: Dux in *G*, bass: Comes in *D*).

The fugue contains no learned complications such
as those of stretto, inversion, augmentation etc., and there‑
fore, so as not to result in a monotonous succession of
theme entries, must make rich use of episode. The
countersubject is strictly carried through:

The following counterpoint to the countersubject apart
from the theme entries, occurs in the first episode

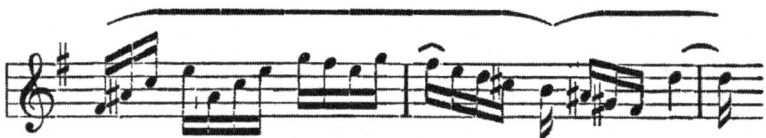

and further use of it is made later on. Entirely new ma‑
terial is developed in the second episode

which likewise recurs.

The chief sections are: 1. Exposition: 2 8-measure periods; first Dux (*E-minor—B-minor*) in the soprano, and then Comes (*B-minor—F♯-major*) in the bass; the episode which follows concludes in G.

·2. Modulation section *a*) Dux (G—D) in the soprano; Comes (D—A) in the bass; an episode modulates through C-*major* to A-*minor* (with a remarkable *unisono* of both voices);

b) Dux (*A-minor — E-minor*) in the bass, Comes (*E-minor—B*) in the soprano; an episode modulates to *D-minor*;

c) Dux (*D-minor — A-minor*) in the bass, Comes (*A-minor — E*) in the soprano; another episode ($c^7 - {}^0c$ [$=c^6$] — $d^7 — g^+ — b^7$ [*unisono*]) finally leads to

3. The concluding section in the principal key, which only consists of 4 measures: dux in the soprano, and then, once more Dux, commenced in the bass, but completed in the soprano.

I. 11.

PRELUDE AND FUGUE IN F-MAJOR.

These two pieces, as suggested by the character of the key, are clear and simple. The prelude is strictly written in two voices nearly all the way through and (with exception of two bars) might quite well be classed among the 2-part "Inventions", to which, in its whole structure, it bears a strong resemblance. Its contents, *i. e.* the vital power revealed in the movement of the melody, in rhythm and harmony, or, if we consider the form, the esthetic effect of the piece might be defined as active industry without haste; the bright key of F-*major* sparkles like morning fresh with dew, and even the key of D-*minor*, which appears in conjunction with it, remains free from all bitterness and melancholy, for its most powerful harmonies (the chords of B♭-*major* and A-*major*) are selected by preference. The first two measures give out the motive from which the whole piece is developed:

Allegretto vivace (♩.).

(2)

In the after-section of this period there appears a new element, viz. a shake with fore-slide (Vorschleife) and after-beat (Nachschlag)

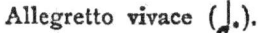

.

The great distance (3 octaves!) between the two voices is extraordinary; towards the close the under one descends to the lowest (C), and the upper one to the highest (c^3) note of the keyboard of Bach's time. The following is the harmonic scheme: —

i. e. a short period (4 measures ♩. | ♩.) forming the ground work firmly establishes the key of *F*; a second (eight measures) modulates to *D-minor* and settles firmly in that key; a third, which is approached by a general up-beat*) of 2 ♩. (the triplet ♩. ♩. ♩. should be noticed!) modulates through *A-major* and *G-major* (!) to *Bb-major*; a fourth passes through *G-minor* back to *F-major*, and firmly establishes this key in the after-section; whereupon, after a brief transition passage (general up-beat but without triplet formation, and only the 8th measure changing its meaning to that of 1st), the introductory short period (4 measures ♩. | ♩.) returns (theme in the lower voice), an appended and extended cadence bringing the whole to a conclusion.

The fugue (à 3), although it contains strettos, is one of the simplest and least pretentious. Pleasantly does the theme move between fifth and fundamental note, touching besides, the upper and under neighbouring degrees. The opportunity may here be taken to refer to an idea of

---

*) A general up-beat is not a single up-beat to the following motive, but a transition or group leading to the phrase or theme which follows.

Felix Dräseke's, to which I attach special importance, viz.
not to regard the octave 1—8 as the harmonic scheme
for melody movement, but rather the tonic triad with the
two boundary degrees; thus for F-major,

not: but:

For, as not only Moritz Hauptmann, but even Guido
d'Arrezzo felt (as, indeed, can be seen from his system which
resulted in solmisation), from the 6th to the 7th degree of
the key a gap is perceptible, to cross over which means
nothing less than a *transition to another region of the
domain of sounds.* For themes of narrow compass, such
as those of most fugues, it naturally makes a very great
difference, whether they remain in one tone region, or
whether they rise, or sink to another. The character of
contemplative repose, which the themes of the *C-major,
C♯-minor, D-minor* and *E♭-minor* fugues must be acknow-
ledged to possess, is owing, and in no small degree, to this
consideration. The theme of the *D-major* fugue is too
impulsive in rhythm, to be regarded as of quiet character:
the hurried leap up to the sixth in it appears like an
attempt to force, with violence, a passage across the above-
mentioned gap. Our present theme is at first comfortably
poised on the fifth, like a fish resting on the top of a
smooth wave: it then dives below the fundamental note,
glides back again to the fifth, and then with quiet serpentine motion passes through the third down to the fundamental note;

and, as if Bach had really been influenced by an associa-
tion of ideas similar to the one hinted at here, the voice,
continuing as counterpoint while the Comes is given out,
develops at length the serpentine semiquaver movement,
and ends with a shake, which in this connection has a
specially striking effect

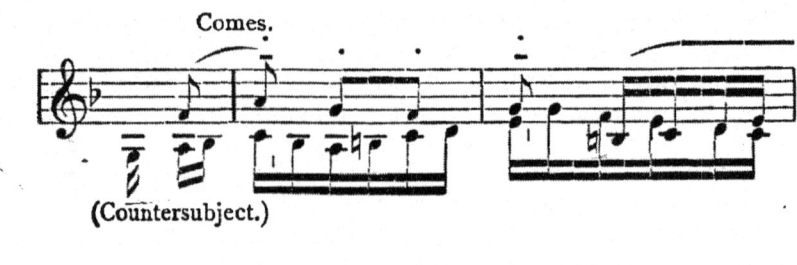

The answer only differs from the theme in the first step (*f—a* instead of *g—a* answering to *c—d*), not so much to satisfy a (non-existent) principle that tonic should be answered by dominant at the outset, but rather, indeed (as in the *C♯-major*-fugue), to enable the Comes to *modulate to the key of the dominant from the tonic*, and not, after the conclusion in the principal key, to spring to that of the dominant:

The fugue spins along without formality, revelling in the full freedom of its melody. The third voice (bass) does not enter immediately (although that could have been accomplished without difficulty), but only after an inserted free measure which inclines towards the principal key (c^7—f^+) and permits the upper voice to proceed quietly to rest; under the concluding notes comes the new entry (8a=1) at the end of which the exposition (collecting of all the voices and production of the thematic material) must be considered at an end (three periods of four measures). The first (principal) section (the one in the principal key) extends beyond the exposition, and comprises a second, and indeed, redundant development with the following order of voices, soprano (Dux), alto (Comes), bass (Dux), and in stretto with the bass once more the alto (Comes); between these first two developments there is an episode of four measures, which, with a syncopated counterpoint (of which no further use is made), rises to the dominant, while the bass has the countersubject. This counter-subject appears, besides, with all the seven theme entries of the principal section, faithfully accompanying the theme (but *Comes* [companion] ought really to be the name of the first counterpoint, in so far as it is retained, rather than that of the "answer").

The already mentioned stretto at the end of the first section requires a close-confirmation of two measures, from which, by a delayed resolution of the ninth (g) springs an episode leading to the (modulating) middle section

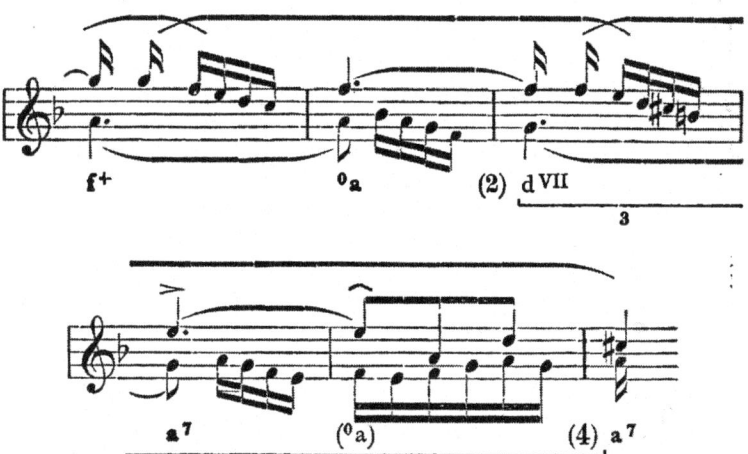

(under the last notes is heard the beginning of the theme in the bass ($c\sharp$ d c $b\flat$ a).

The middle (modulating) section is likewise capable of being subdivided: after the half close on a^7 there is first, a strict stretto of the theme in *D-minor* (all three voices: soprano, alto and bass beginning with a $b\flat$); and, until the bass makes its entry with the theme, it holds on to a as an organ-point. The second half of the middle section, which follows on without modulation after a close-confirmation of two measures, is in *G-minor*, and consists of a stretto of

all three voices in reversed order (bass, alto, soprano, beginning with *d—e♭*).   All the strettos (including the one
with which the first section closes) are formed by the second half of the theme acting as counterpoint to the first
half. of the same

The concluding section — the self-evident return to
and re-establishment of the principal key, is specially
remarkable in that it does not contain a single complete
theme entry. The return is effected in the simplest manner
(^0d [$=b♭^6$] $—c^7—f^+$), and the continuation, by introduction
of the natural seventh of the tonic ($7♮ = e♭$) touches, in
well-known fashion, the key of the under-dominant (cadences: $f^7—b♭^+$ and $c^7—f^+$). The rhythm of both halves
of the theme (quaver movement by degrees, and serpentine semiquaver movement) continues during the whole
of the concluding section, but the integral theme is
not once to be met with; only once does it seem as if
it would present itself in stable shape:

But there the matter rests; in place of the swinging on the
fifth and the quiet movement within one tone region,
there runs through the whole of the concluding section a
scale movement in quavers pressing forward in a straight
line, while the winding of the semiquaver movement
opposed to the same increases in extent. Returning to
the metaphor used at the commencement of our analysis,
we no longer see the sleek dwellers in the watery element
playing in the sunlight on the surface, but quietly gliding
in the depths, now downwards, now upwards; a picture of
peace, on which we gaze, until the final cadence removes
it from sight.

I. 12.

PRELUDE AND FUGUE IN F-MINOR.

The key of *F-minor* — sombre both by its minor character, and by its position on the undertone side of the fundamental scale (key of the under-third of *A-minor*) — yet, standing in close relationship to the fundamental major scale (*C*), and commanding the C-major chord as dominant, it receives a consoling ray of light — is one of the most melancholy of keys. It does not express sorrow as deep as that of *E♭-minor*, nor passion as morbid as that of *C♯-minor*, but it is impregnated with deeper feeling, greater solemnity, pensiveness, introspection, than almost any other key. Its near relationship to *C-major* (the *F-minor*-chord is the counter-clang, the Antipodes of the *C-major*-chord) gives to it the character of one standing in the world, yet with averted eyes. Quiet and unerring he advances with head erect through the crowd, intently surveying everything, but, like a true philosopher, not heeding small things. Place side by side the first movement of Beethoven's *Appassionata* and the *F-minor* prelude of the first part of the Well-tempered Clavier, and in both the same features will be quickly recognized!

The characteristic elements of the prelude are a motive wandering slowly along in uniform crotchets (for the most part simultaneously, in two voices) and, in opposition to it, and lighting up its countenance, an expressive semiquaver figuration interspersed with significant (accented) rests. The piece is, for the most part, written strictly à 4; the figuration is absent from the bass, which, when not advancing earnestly in crotchets, generally has notes of greater value — at the beginning, a short organ-point on the tonic, and at the end, a long one on the dominant. The motive material is stated at the opening:

Sostenuto e cantabile.

(4)

The harmonic construction (with the essence of the melody which, for the most part, is broken up into figures) is as follows: —

The first period keeps in *F-minor*, making a half close in that key; the second modulates to *Ab-major* (parallel), the third goes to *C-minor* and to *C-major* (upper-dominant), the fourth turns through *Bb-minor* back to *F-minor*, while the fifth (the last) brings back the opening period (but with decidedly greater emphasis), and stands over a dominant organ-point. Three times (at [v]) accented measures (8., 4) change meaning and become unaccented (5., 1.).

The fugue (à 4), in deep musing, stands not a whit behind the prelude; by its theme the measured movement of uniform crotchets becomes also here a characteristic feature:

Adagio pensieroso.

Although already the countersubject introduces semi-quaver movement, and although the crotchets are slow enough to represent beats, still the *Allabreve* character of the fugue cannot be ignored. The minims are certainly so slow as to produce the character of measured movement, which, by the constantly recurring runs of the counter-subject (typical of the whole figuration of the long piece), becomes all the more prominent:

Countersubject.

The straight lines of the separate motives should be well noted; where a feminine ending would cause the bending of a line, the "ligature" (syncopation) is replaced by a rest, and the end note becomes the starting note of a new motive. Thus it is impossible to lose sight of the already emphasized Allabreve-character of the theme and to bring out the same in performance, without allowing the small details of a highly expressive figuration to obscure it (herein the fugue differs essentially from the prelude, which has not also this Allabreve-character).

The answer of the theme is quite analogous to that of the *F-major* fugue; here, as there, the theme commences with the fifth of the scale (but in the harmony of the tonic) and ends on the fundamental note; the Comes has therefore to modulate from the harmony of the tonic to the key of the dominant *i. e.* the answer does not commence with *g*, but with *f*, so that the first melodic step is extended. The chromatic nature of the theme is faithfully preserved in the answer; it implies harmonic depths, which materially aid in bringing out the pensive character of this fugue:

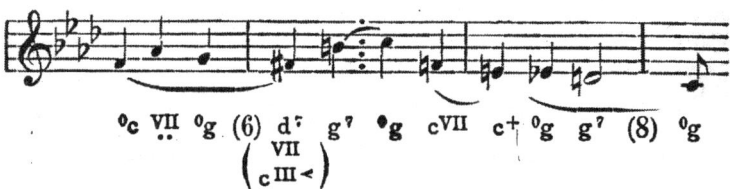

$$^{o}c \ \underset{..}{VII} \ ^{o}g \ (6) \ d^{7} \ g^{7} \ ^{\bullet}g \ cVII \ c^{+} \ ^{o}g \ g^{7} \ (8) \ ^{o}g$$
$$\left(\underset{cIII \prec}{VII}\right)$$

The metrical nature of the theme (– ◡ –; the 1st [unaccented] measure is wanting) gives rise to a great number of elisions (whenever an entry of the theme occurs, a measure of 4 crotchets or 2 minims is wanting). If, in spite of this, the symmetry never appears seriously to be disturbed, and changes of meaning (of measures) do not occur, the reason is that, as soon as the theme ceases, in place of the above mentioned Allabreve measure, an ordinary ⁴/₄ bar (with crotchets as beats or counts) enters; for it is certainly clearly impossible to take the episodes with their logical working-out of the first motive of the counter-subject (♪♪ ❘ ♩), in an Allabreve-sense.

We have therefore throughout the fugue alternate periods, some with the measure motive ♩ ❘ ♩, others with ♩ ❘ ♩.

The first development includes the 4 voice entries in the order, tenor — alto, — bass — soprano: of these the first three (Dux — Comes — Dux) are immediately connected one with the other, whereas between the third and the fourth, an episode of 6 measures ♩ ❘ ♩ (1—2; 1a—2a; 3—4) is inserted. The fourth voice brings in likewise the Dux, so that the exposition concludes in the principal key (total compass; 3 times 3 measures of ♩ ❘ ♩, 6 measures of ♩ ❘ ♩, and still once more 3 measures of ♩ ❘ ♩).

The second development, likewise in the principal key, is of looser construction, and contains only two theme-entries. After an episode of 6 measures ♩ | ♩, modulating to *C-minor* (1—4, 3 a—4 a), the tenor introduces the theme in the key of the upper-dominant (*C-minor*) or rather — the Comes without its distinctive mark (the third at the commencement), and after a new episode leading back through *B♭-minor* and *A♭-major* to *F-minor*, and consisting of 8 measures ♩ | ♩, with emphatic repetition of the first group of the after section (triplet of ♩ | ♩ measures), the bass introduces the Dux, at the conclusion of which, by cessation (though only quite a short one) of the three upper voices, the close of the first (principal) section is marked off.

The modulating *middle* section again has only two theme entries, first in the alto, after an episode of 8 measures ♩ | ♩ passing through *D♭-major*, *B♭-minor* to *A♭-major*; this entry commences in *A♭-major*, but the close turns to *F-minor* (everything indeed happens so smoothly and so naturally that I cannot discover in it any trace of Bruyck's "harmonic egg dance" ["harmonischer Eiertanz"]); and, after a further episode of 7 measures ♩ | ♩ (the first, an unaccented one, is passed over), which modulates through *C-minor* and *A♭-major* to *E♭-major* (half close on bb^7), a second in the tenor. With this the end of the middle section is reached *i. e.* the next episode, which passes through *A♭-major*, and *F-minor* (principal key) to a *half close on g^7, leads already to the*

Concluding section (re-establishment of the principal key). The chief features of the latter are the appearance of the theme which now follows in the key of the dominant (*C-minor*), or better still of the Comes without the distinction only necessary for the first development; and, after an intermediate episode, of 6 measures ♩ | ♩ the appearance of the Dux in the bass, to which, finally, a close-confirmation of 4 measures ♩ | ♩ is appended. Thus the tripartite division is here easily recognized and the modulatory means are altogether of a simple character; so that, throughout, the principal key of *F-minor* forms the point of stress.

I. 13.

PRELUDE AND FUGUE IN F-SHARP.

The nature-painting moods of the *C-sharp* and *E-major* preludes have new noble counterparts in this prelude and the fugue of similar mood which follows. As the key of *F-sharp* stands between *E-major* and *C♯-major*, brighter than the former but less glowing than the latter (compare the passage in F♯ in the middle of the C♯ prelude), so does the F♯ prelude form a natural middle member between the one in E, fresh as spring, and the other in C♯, rich with summer glow. Although strictly in two voices from beginning to end, still it is full of life, entrancing up to the very last note, moving onward in so natural a manner, that one always lingers over it with renewed rapture. The gently swinging opening motive (afterwards with short shake on the concluding note)

which is immediately taken up by the under voice, at once calls to mind the mood of the prelude in E. This indeed is the only figuration motive which the under voice repeats alternately with the upper one: the former proceeds quietly, in ♪ counts, by diatonic steps — in long descending and ascending lines, producing an effect similar to that of the ♩ movement in the *C♯-major* prelude — while the upper voice carries out a syncopated motive of enchanting grace:

while listening to it one can only think of the woods, of flowers, and of the song of birds. The close-confirmation which occurs four times, forms an especially refined feature:

(8a)

We may venture to pass over a detailed harmonic analysis of this piece: it offers no intricate problem. We only give a general outline of the construction.

The introductory motive first quoted above offers a point of support of highest order (8th measure), from which the first period is regularly evolved, terminating on the dominant ($c\sharp^+$). On the concluding note of the close-confirmation, the motive recommences; at first we have the 8th measure above mentioned as point of support (notice well the feeling of repose thus obtained), and then the upper voice descends again with the syncopated motive; but the under-dominant of $C\sharp$-*major* ($f\sharp^6$) which is reached in the second measure changes its meaning to that of minor tonic ($^0a\sharp$) in that it begins again (a 5th lower), so that the first group (1st and 2nd measures), with changed harmonic contents, is repeated (1a—2a); the key of $D\sharp$-*minor* (parallel) is now adhered to until the close of this period. The next period, in the fore-section, turns to the key of $A\sharp$-*minor* (parallel of the upper-dominant), and in the after-section to $G\sharp$-*minor* (parallel of the under-dominant); this must be looked upon as the modulating middle section as in the following period $^0d\sharp$ changes its meaning to b^6, and already in the fore-section concludes in $F\sharp$-*major*, which is now adhered to to the end (still through another and complete period).

The fugue (à 3) is as pleasing and as graceful as the prelude. It is important to note that the theme sinks down from the octave, through the fifth and third, to the fundamental note (cf. our remarks on the theme of the fugue in *F-major*):

6*

Andantino quasi Allegretto.

It can scarcely be by chance that Bach chose a corresponding order of entry of voices (soprano — alto — bass), so that not only within the separate theme entries, but through the whole exposition the esthetic impression remains the same (an inward down-sinking): Yes, it is not difficult to recognize that this tendency prevails throughout the whole fugue. It is also worthy of note how Bach suppresses the feminine ending (third — fundamental note) in both the bass entries of the theme, thus attracting, on both occasions, special attention to the end of the downward movement. In the answer to the theme the intervals are faithfully maintained with exception of the opening step in which to 5—1 is opposed, according to rule, 1—5 of the key, thereby satisfying the oft repeated principle, that when the Dux remains in the principal key, the Comes must modulate from tonic harmony to key of the dominant, and not leap to the same.

The counterpoint of the first voice which accompanies the Comes:

countersubject:

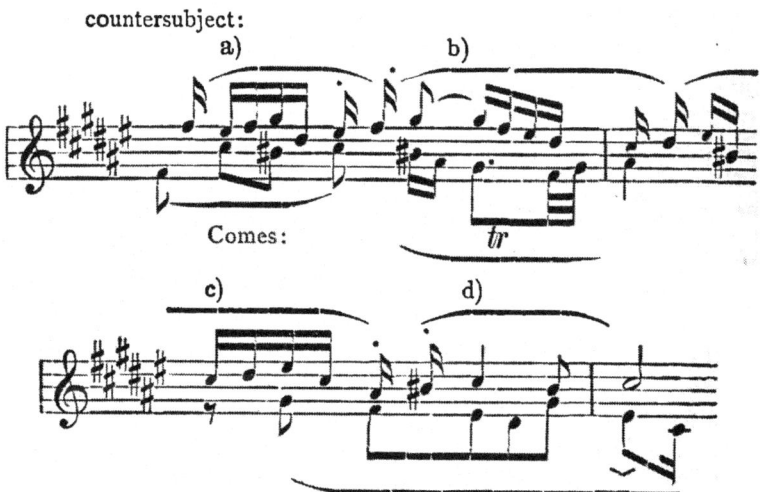

appears, with two exceptions, against all the theme entries, but transposed not only in double counterpoint of the octave, but also twice in that of the twelfth (but only from motive *b*) thus: —

double counterpoint in the 8^{ve}.

double counterpoint in the 8^{ve}   double counterpoint in the 12th

in the 8^{ve}   :   in the 12th

This counter-subject clings closely to the theme, and offers but little resistance to the downward tendency of the latter, nay, rather is drawn down with it.

Perhaps it may have been Bach's intention to disturb as little as possible, by other formations, the impression of the theme peacefully descending through the three voices. Only the episode following the exposition introduces a new characteristic motive which afterwards consorts with the theme and countersubject, and, in fact, becomes a real second counter-subject; it has a light upward motion, almost as if it were a body without weight capable of being raised by the gentlest breath of air, and incapable of a real fall.

Its character is first fully shown where the soprano —
contrary to all custom — begins the second development
in the same position as that of the first, and indeed with
the Dux: —

Also in this second development the theme runs
through the voices from top to bottom (alto: Comes —
without the distinction in the opening step, thus: theme in
$C\sharp$-*major*; bass: theme in $D\sharp$-*minor*). At the second entry
(alto) the new counter-subject is wanting; at the third, after
a modest start, the first countersubject gives place to it
entirely, when it appears in inverted form, and already
ascends this time up to $d\sharp^2$, while in the last development
it climbs up as high as b^2. We must not attempt to
pursue in detail the alternate play of the motive of the
theme, of the first, and especially of the second countersubject. The number of theme entries is only a small
one, also in the concluding section there are only two —
one in the alto: Dux in the under-dominant, and one in
the soprano; Dux for the third time in the same position
as at the opening (the theme is also drawn upwards in
the concluding section by the second countersubject); but
the opening motive of the theme is on the move at all
ends and corners (at the beginning of the concluding
section it is given out four times, alternately by soprano
and alto, and then descends four times by degrees in the
bass), so that it sounds as if there were many entries or
strettos.

The order of modulation is as follows: — 1st section
(exposition): twofold modulation to the key of the dominant,
which, however, both times, by addition of the seventh,
again becomes dominant harmony. The second (modulating) section turns, first from the principal key to the

key of the dominant, and then to the parallel key. The 3rd section returns from the last named key to the principal one, and through this to the key of the underdominant, finally keeping firmly to the principal key. Here again the simplest means, most easy of comprehension, are employed and yet what enchanting effect does not the master evolve from them!

I. 14.
PRELUDE AND FUGUE IN F♯-MINOR.

The mood of both these pieces is elegiacal; still, with respect to depth of feeling, there is a marked difference between them. The prelude especially is related to the parallel key, the clear, joyous one of *A-major*, and in the whole of its motive material is of lighter formation than the fugue — dragging along with notes of long values and syncopations, and avoiding almost intentionally the key of *A-major* —, and gravitates rather towards the passionate one of *C♯-minor*. Perhaps one ought to look upon the prelude as landscape, on the fugue as soul-painting; in both it is the season of autumn, but while the autumn mood of nature casts, as it were, only a light shadow over the landscape —, it is only a change of forms, the passing-away is an opening to new life — through the fugue runs a solemn awe — the question: to be or not to be!

The principal design of the prelude is an undulating movement in semiquavers, which sinks from the sixth to the fundamental note:

In addition, over a stationary bass, the middle voice gives short notes descending in parallel movement — are they drops of rain, or tears?

Both motives dominate the whole piece; the second is frequently modified (as already in the very next measure), so that by breaking up of a voice part even the inter- mediate quaver values produce a similar effect:

or even so, that in the feminine ending ($\frown$) of the principal motive the "dropping" tones appear as semi- quavers in the same voice part:

The feminine ending of the principal motive dis- appears — not reckoning the stereotyped close-formulae appended to the several sectional closes — only once, by means of 2 double measures ($^4/_4$), giving place to a smooth- ly running motive with masculine ending

they are, however, only a leading-back, and immediately precede a cadence.

The structure is as follows: —

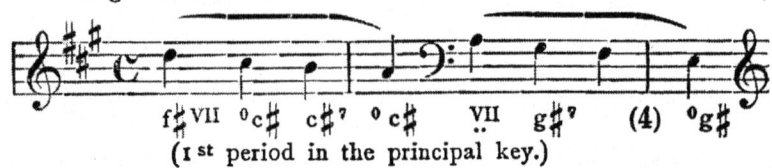

(1st period in the principal key.)

(2nd period modulating to the parallel key and in the after-section to the dominant.)

(close-confirmation)

(cadence)

c♯VII °g♯ g♯⁷ °g♯   c♯VII °g♯ g♯⁷ (4) °g♯
(b III◄)

(3rd period leading in the after section to the under-dominant and parallel keys.)

f♯⁷ °f♯ f♯⁷   °f♯   e⁷ a⁺ e⁷ (8) a⁺ ‖
(= d°)

d⁺   6̈   c♯⁷ °c♯ f♯VII c♯⁷   (4) °c♯ ‖
(= f♯ VII)
(leading back)

‖ f♯VII ..   (4a) c♯⁷ ‖ f♯VII °c♯ c♯⁷   °c♯
(Cadence)   (Concluding period in principal key.)

f♯VII °c♯ c♯⁷ (4) °c♯ c♯⁷ °c♯ f♯VII c♯⁷ (4a) °c♯
(Cadence)

f♯VII °c♯ c♯⁷ °c♯ f♯VII °c♯ c♯⁷ (8) °c♯ f♯VII c♯⁷ f♯⁺(1)
(Cadence)

The theme of the fugue (à 4) passes slowly upward from the fundamental note to the third, and, amid pain and torture, struggles still further with chromatic harmonies up to the fifth, from which it sinks back by degrees to the fundamental tone.

"Scholastic and heavy" ("Scholastisch schwerfällig"), "grave rather than pathetic" ("mehr gravitätisch als pathetisch") is the way in which Bruyck describes this fugue, and he speaks of the "halting members" ("stockende Glieder") of the theme. It almost seems to me as if he had not quite understood the harmony on which it is based, so that this remnant of non-comprehension spoilt his enjoyment of the piece, certainly one of highly complicated character. The metrical nature of the theme with its twofold presentation of the second measure (2, 2a, 2b) is decidedly not one of the easiest to understand. The harmonic meaning of the theme — as is always the case with Bach — is definitely fixed by the first countersubject: the latter is given here with the Comes (which is an exact transposition of the Dux into the dominant)

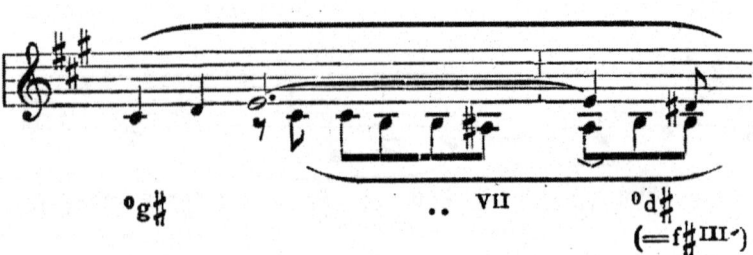

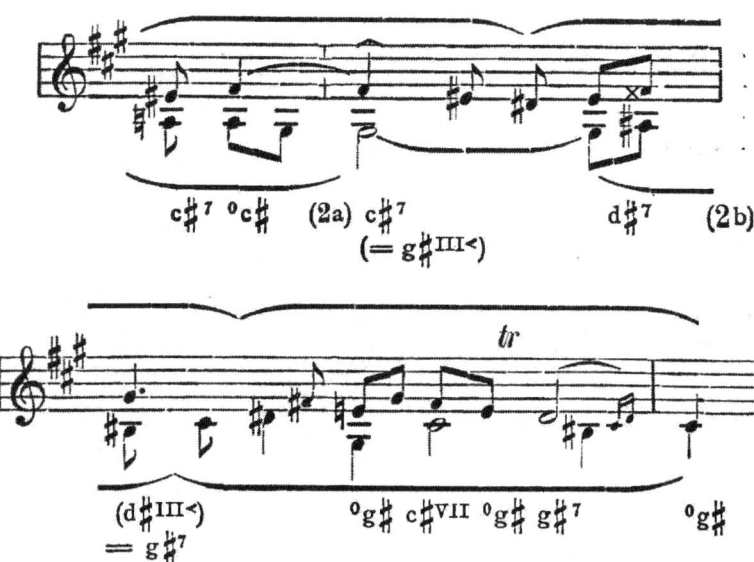

thus we twice meet with the interval of the Doric sixth; *i. e.* twice a consonant clang-element, owing to an unexpected chromatic progression, is further changed to the Doric sixth ($d\sharp$ is I in $^{o}d\sharp$, but $3^{<}$ in b^{+}; $e\sharp$ is 3 in $c\sharp^{+}$). A third 3 ($b\sharp$) occurs in place of an expected III, and turns the minor tonic chord into a major upper-dominant. That such super-abundance of harmony requires slow *tempo*, is self-evident; if time be not given to the ear to grasp the idea of the various (chromatic) notes which create surprise, part of the meaning will, of necessity, remain concealed. The actual length of the fugue is therefore moderate (only nine theme entries [not eight, as Jadassohn makes out]). The strong modulation within the theme enables one to dispense with modulation other than that which is required to prepare the later entries of the theme in the key of the dominant. A real tripartite division, such as we are accustomed to find, can with difficulty be traced here, at least, not from the order of modulation. If the first foundation-laying section be considered as extending to the end of the theme entry of the fourth voice (soprano), the boundary between the first and second sections is not clearly marked off; and it appears astonishing that two voices (bass and soprano) — separated, besides, by a long episode — should introduce, one after the other, the

Dux. For these reasons it seems to me right to consider the first (principal) section as extending only up to the entry of the soprano, *i. e.* to the end of the 8-measure episode which follows the bass entry, and where occurs a leaning — and the only one — towards the parallel key (*A-major*). If above I laid emphasis on the almost intentional avoidance of this (parallel) key, I may here add that this key, by the introduction of the *G-major* chord at the beginning of the sequence closing in *A-major*, is marked, as it were, with a feeling of deep pain (2nd underdominant, a chord of the Neapolitan 6th in a twice-transmitted sense: g^+ as $^0f\sharp^{2>}$, where $^0f\sharp$ itself $= d^6$). A second boundary (the line of division between the middle and the concluding section) is, to a certain extent, marked off by the pause in tenor and bass at the close in *C♯-minor* (they both re-enter, successively, with the theme). The episodes agree altogether with the character of the theme and of the countersubject, and are evolved mostly from the third motive of the theme,

and from the syncopation belonging to the first, and to the second motive. The countersubject faithfully accompanies the theme, and is also repeatedly employed in the episodes. In the inversion of the theme only the characteristic wavy movement is to be recognized in the counterpoint, but no strict carrying out of the same, although that would have been quite possible

That Bach made no use of this combination, is a sufficient answer to all insinuations about "scholasticism" and "manufacture" ("Mache"). The introduction of the inversion of the theme presents itself as a thoroughly natural consequence, and all the more as the theme thoroughly preserves its character; one might say that in place of painful upward striving, there was here greater inwardness, a deeper sinking into self. Besides the above inversion, which the alto introduces in the middle section, Bach gives a second form in the bass in the concluding section: it begins and ends with $f\sharp$, and probably must be regarded as the inversion of the Dux, as the former that of the Comes. The fugue contains theme entries in no other keys than those of $F\sharp$-*minor* (Dux) and $C\sharp$-*minor* (Comes). That preference was given in the concluding section to the Dux and its inversion just as in the middle section to the Comes and its inversion, was a logical consequence, where, as here, there was absence of real digression.

With regard to the melodic outline, it may be specially pointed out, that Bach keeps the first section in a low position (even the second soprano entry does not go above $c\sharp^2$), and only adopts a higher position in the middle section. The fugue, like the prelude, ends in a conciliatory manner in $F\sharp$-*major*.

I. 15.

PRELUDE AND FUGUE IN G-MAJOR.

Both pieces are as brisk as bees: the prelude has throughout gay semiquaver-triplet-figuration, while the fugue, in most lively ⁶/₈ time, runs its course for the most part in smooth semiquaver motion. The *tempo* of both is somewhat rapid, the character throughout one of untroubled joy, of lively enjoyment. Was Bach really conscious of the fact that the prelude in *G-major* was related to the one in $C\sharp$-*major*? There is certainly not such glowing heat here as there: it is not midsummer, but spring, young fresh spring (it should also be compared

with the preludes in E and F); but, as there, so here, we meet
with the same sensible, thoughtful human being who revels
in the enjoyment of nature. The slender arpeggio motive
of the first measures recalls the prelude in *E-major*:

Allegro risoluto.

but already the close of the first little period with its
persistent *c♯—d* carries us back to the prelude in *C♯-major*:

and with good reason, for an old friend, reclining amidst
the tall grass, is gazing at us:

in the *C-sharp* prelude

And now let each see for himself whether he does not discover many other kindred features (the octave leaps of the lower voice, and especially the whole jugglery of the light-winged figuration); only here everything is more precipitate, more impulsive, springing - forth, fluttering and bounding: it is, in fact, youthful spring!

The piece requires no analysis; the harmonies are as clear as daylight, and the order of keys is normal (principal key, dominant, parallel, dominant, under-dominant, principal key).

The Fugue (à 3) carries on a truly jesting game with a somewhat long and prolix theme, which, first of all, rolls upward in merry circular movement from the fundamental note to the third degree, and then, with wanton leaps from the under-fourth and under-leading-note, extends beyond the fifth:

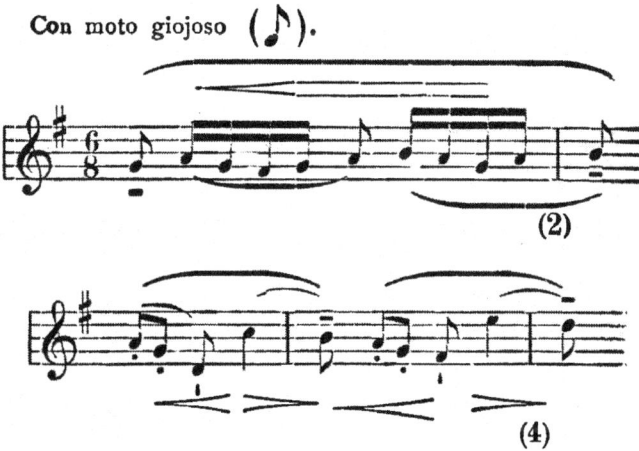

The countersubject opposed to it first runs downward to the third of the dominant, then, so long as the Comes (which is only a transposition of the Dux in the fifth)

moves in a circle, proceeds leisurely in quavers, but afterwards rolls upward in lively fashion to the octave:

Three free measures inserted between the second and
third entries of the theme introduce a fresh motive, which
afterwards attains to considerable importance (movement by
degrees with a note always sounding betwixt and between):

and, by way of contrast, we have an interesting syncopated
motive in the following episode:

Nearly the whole of the material which serves for
the working out of this fugue has now been shown (all
the motives are combined in all sorts of ways, and also
treated in inversion).

In the exposition the theme appears in the three voices
(soprano, alto, bass), during which, it naturally occurs in
the dominant key (Comes), but concludes in the principal

one, to which the transition to the second development adheres. This also remains in the principal key: here we have the *theme in inversion* accompanied by the *countersubject in inversion*, worked out in the following order: — alto (Dux [beginning on *d*]), soprano (Comes (beginning on *a*]), bass (Dux), and, indeed, without any connecting bars thrown in. Thus the first section forming the basis comes to a close.

The second (modulating) section begins with an episode of six measures, which, passing through *A-minor*, modulates to *E-minor* (parallel): in its second half it has only two voices (the alto ceases). The next development is incomplete; the theme first occurs in the soprano in the key of *E-minor*, and is only accompanied in its second half by the counter-subject; then follows the inversion (likewise in *E-minor*, but from *g*) accompanied by the counter-subject in the soprano, whereupon comes a fresh episode effecting modulation to *B-minor* (parallel of the dominant key). The second portion of the modulating section introduces first a *stretto* of the theme between the soprano and bass in *B-minor* (alto ceases):

8 ve lower.

and after an episode of six measures modulating back to *D-major*, a second one, at the same interval, in the key of *D* between alto and soprano, in the course of which the bass remains stationary on *a*; the soprano ends with a shake on *e* (harmony *a*⁷, triplet of 3 ♩.), and three more free measures lead to a broad close in *D-major*, strengthened by a cadence. This close proves to be the beginning of the final section (in the principal key), for on the last note the soprano begins a long shake on *d*, while the bass takes up the theme in the key of *G-major*, and in inversion (from *d*), ending on *g* (the alto again accompanies with the countersubject in inversion).

But in order to make clear the coda-character of this section, the bass, leaving out a half measure, springs down to the low C (the lowest note of the keyboard in those days), and the music turns to the key of the under-dominant (C), quickly passing, however, through *A-minor* and *a⁷* to the dominant (half-close on the low D); in addition the last stretto begins, changing the meaning of the 8ᵗʰ measure to that of 1ˢᵗ, but it is not strictly carried out. First of all the alto starts from *d* with the inverted theme, and after one measure the bass follows with the same; but as soon as the soprano (in the following measure) introduces the theme in its original form, commencing on the 3ʳᵈ (b), the alto gives up the inversion, and first of all joins the soprano in third-doubling, while the bass, instead of the second half of the inverted theme, continues the circular movement downwards as counter-part to that of the two upper voices. The remainder forms a free cadence in *G-major*, with the last four measures over the bass remaining stationary on *g.*

I. 16.

PRELUDE AND FUGUE IN G-MINOR.

I must take this prelude under my special protection against Bruyck; for although the same defends both the prelude and fugue against Forkel, still he comes to the conclusion that the prelude is somewhat angular ("etwas Eckiges"), that the shake organ-point in the third measure does not sound overpleasantly ("dass der Triller-Orgelpunkt im dritten Takte nicht zum lieblichsten klinge"), that in these pieces "angular forms and figures express a certain burlesque humour" ("eckigen Formen und Figuren ein gewisser burlesker Humor ausdrucke"),and that certain hard effects in the after-section of the last period were pet fads of Bach. I cannot agree with a single one of those remarks; I find neither angular points nor hard effects, neither humour nor burlesque in the piece. Evidently Bruyck came to grief here through incorrect reading;

7 *

and that may have happened not only to him and Forkel, but to many another. I select only the passages standing in question, which indeed give a satisfactory idea of the general contents. The "not overpleasantly sounding shake-organ-point" is as follows: —

Where, in this, is there the slightest disturbance of the euphony? The *g* belongs to all the harmonies as chord note, and the suspensions (*d c*, *b♭ a* and *b♭ c* over chord of *g*VII) are perfectly easy to understand, and, if only played properly (with a certain dwelling on the notes marked ⌒ [agogic accent]), produce an excellent effect.

I cannot discover Bruyck's *progression of sevenths* in the following passage:

while the passage, apparently most repugnant to Bruyck,

if only rightly understood (especially the chord of the Neapolitan sixth with its ornamented suspension), is not only full of expression and pathos, but entirely free from harsh effects. In order to be grasped by the listener, it must be rendered in a broad manner.

The whole piece is of a contemplative, earnest mood (the tendency to repeated formations of an organ-point character should be noticed), and of a certain power of expression owing to the up-beat form

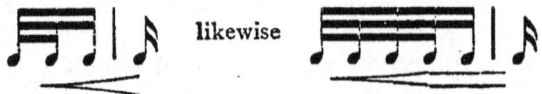

which pervades the whole and in which the running demisemiquavers are brought, as it were, to a standstill against the semiquaver. I presume that no one has been barbarous enough to turn them into mad motives of the following form

which would certainly be angular, burlesque, and indeed humorous!

The structure with regard to key is as follows: —
1st period in *G-minor* with half-close (d^+) at the 8th
measure; the repeated after-section then modulates to
B♭-major (parallel); the 2nd period modulates to *C-minor*
(under-dominant), and at the 4th measure makes a half,
and at the 8th a full-close, which is confirmed (8 *a*). The
3rd period returns by the nearest road ($^0g = g^{\mathrm{VII}}$) to the
principal key, and remains stationary, at the fourth measure,
on a half-close (d^7), which is repeatedly confirmed; also
the full-close of the eighth measure is confirmed by a
supplementary one, with feminine ending, touching on the
under-dominant.

The fugue (à 4) is a highly instructive piece. By the
way it may be mentioned that a Capriccio in *D-minor*
by Friedemann Bach has fugal treatment of a theme almost similar:

Friedemann Bach:

our Dux:

As Friedemann was only twelve years of age when
his father had completed the first part of the Well-tempered
Clavier (1722), his work is probably an unconscious pla-
giarism; but, in every respect, it is inferior to that of his
father's, and especially in the character of the theme
itself, which has lost its pensive earnestness, and has become hurried and restless; the absence of the feminine
ending in the first half, and of the (accented) rest at the
beginning of the second, are heavy losses.

Jadassohn justly notices the unity of the whole fugue,
inasmuch as the countersubject introduces no fresh motive,
but only the inversion of theme motives:

Comes

counter-
subject:

But the matter is not quite so simple as he makes out. Had Bach provided counterpoint somewhat after this fashion:

the countersubject would really be only the inversion of the theme, with the two halves in reversed position, and slight bridging over of the gap; but then the tautology of both would have been unmistakable, and the whole would have been in danger of losing its vitality. Bach, indeed, by using both halves of the theme, but displaced by one crotchet in the measure (so that the accented becomes unaccented, and vice versa), makes *the same thing appear something quite different.* (It is well known that the charm of a close canon consists *in the imitation becoming counter-subject*). If we articulate Bach's countersubject more precisely, we find first a *syncopated motive* (the g before the rest produces an effect quite similar to a note held over, only more striking, more sobbing), which in the feminine ending beyond the rest contains a second element foreign to the theme:

The ascending motive [music notation] at the beginning of the second half, is likewise a very precious addition, as it clearly shows the meaning of the accented rest in the theme, and prevents the same from being understood as an end rest; the inversion of the opening motive has the same position in the measure as in the theme, but arranged so that here it forms the conclusion, whereas there it formed the opening; and thus it, too, forms an important countersubject. By comparing both principal motives through both voices, my meaning will be better understood: —

and:

The theme consists of three measures (– ◡ –) and therefore gives opportunity in the developments for the elision of the unaccented opening measure of the several half periods (1st and 5th M.), whereas the episodes are regularly formed (cf. the *C-major* fugue I. 1). In point of melody the theme belongs to the quiet ones, those based on the triad position (compass $f\sharp$ | g $b\flat$ d | $e\flat$). In the answer a change of interval is seen at the outset (third g $b\flat$ in place of second a $b\flat$), because the Comes has to modulate from the principal key to the dominant, but must not leap at one bound to the same. The first two voice entries (alto, soprano) are separated from the two others (bass, tenor) by an episode of two measures evolved from the countersubject. After the close in *D-minor* (dominant) follows a long episode, with elision of 1st and 5th measures; but it repeats the second group (3—4 M.) and concludes in *B♭-major* (parallel).

The second (modulating middle) section which now
begins, first introduces the Dux (alto) in *B♭-major*, then
the strict Comes (bass) passing regularly from *B♭-major* to
F-major, further the Dux (soprano) in *F-major* (or, one
might say, the Comes in *B♭-major* without its distinguishing opening step), so that this whole second development is in *B♭-major.* The first three entries follow with
elision of the unaccented opening measure, the last without
elision, but also without any connecting notes. The second
half of the modulation section (and also the concluding
section) which is approached by two measures leading
to *C-minor* (under-dominant) has only one form of the
theme (that of the Dux), *i. e.* we have fresh confirmation
of the principle that the structure of the first development
is the real cause of the double form of the theme as Dux
and Comes; but it must not be overlooked that the very
widening of the first step in the theme of this fugue
intensifies the expression. The order of voices in the
third development is as follows: — tenor (theme in
C-minor [*g a♭*], soprano (likewise *g a♭*), alto (theme in
G-minor [principal key]), all three following one another
in immediate succession. This whole development (as
also the following episode already belonging to the closing
section) is throughout in three voices (Forkel's reproach of
less perfection may perchance refer to this long departure
from 4 - part writing). The concluding section resumes
the principal key which enters at the close of the 3rd development, and, at the end of an 8-measure period freely
developed from motive *b* (see above), makes a half-close,
and then follows on with an apparent stretto of the Dux
through three voices (soprano, tenor, bass; only the first
part of the theme is used in complete form, the second
is replaced by the counterplay of the countersubject) and
two complete theme entries (Dux in alto and in tenor), in
which 4-part grows to 5-part writing (but only as chords)!

I. 17.

PRELUDE AND FUGUE IN A♭.

A certain thoughtfulness and tenderness of expression distinguish these two pieces. The prelude is frequently depreciated from an esthetic point of view, and this probably arises from lack of comprehension of the rests in the principal theme, and also from want of a satisfactory clue to the structure, as regards periods, of the piece. If the first measure be taken as unaccented, *i. e.* the second as answering to it, and if one read with full measure (from bar-stroke to bar-stroke), the first section is torn into mere disconnected 2-measure shreds. The metrico-rhythmical contents are rather as follows: —

Allegretto poco mosso.

The second period, with which the first section concludes, modulates to the key of the dominant, and opposes a more lively movement to that of the principal thought:

The second section is a fairly faithful reproduction of the first, with inverted voices, but with modulation turned towards the under-side, *i. e.* to the principal key, and from thence towards that of the under-dominant, so that, at the end, the principal key is established without any difficulty. As to the first section, so also to the second is appended a close-confirmation of one measure, but, in addition, a coda of 8 measures and a one-measure confirmation.

The intentional avoidance of the nearest related minor keys deserves note; even the parallel key is scarcely touched (in the coda with the sequence $d\flat^+ - {}^0f$, $c^+ - {}^0c$), and this, in part, explains the joyful repose of the whole piece.

The fugue (à 4) is remarkable in that it has *no real countersubject*, although here canonic conduct of the theme does not, as in the *C-major* fugue, appear to render the same indispensable. It may be pretty safely assumed that the brevity of the theme and its frequent recurrence induced Bach constantly to change the counterpoint instead of adhering to one fixed form; anyhow, just as smooth quaver movement is the special characteristic of the theme subject to variation of every kind, so smooth semiquaver movement in scale form is the common feature of the counterpoint opposed to it. The theme of two measures is of chord nature:

Andantino.

(Alto:)　　　　　　　　　(2)

and remains quietly in the principal key; the answer must therefore modulate from tonic harmony to the key of the dominant, whereby the Comes assumes a shape differing in a marked manner from the Dux:

to this the alto supplies the following counterpoint:

and then, with the bass, in characteristic fashion, completes an interlude of four measures:

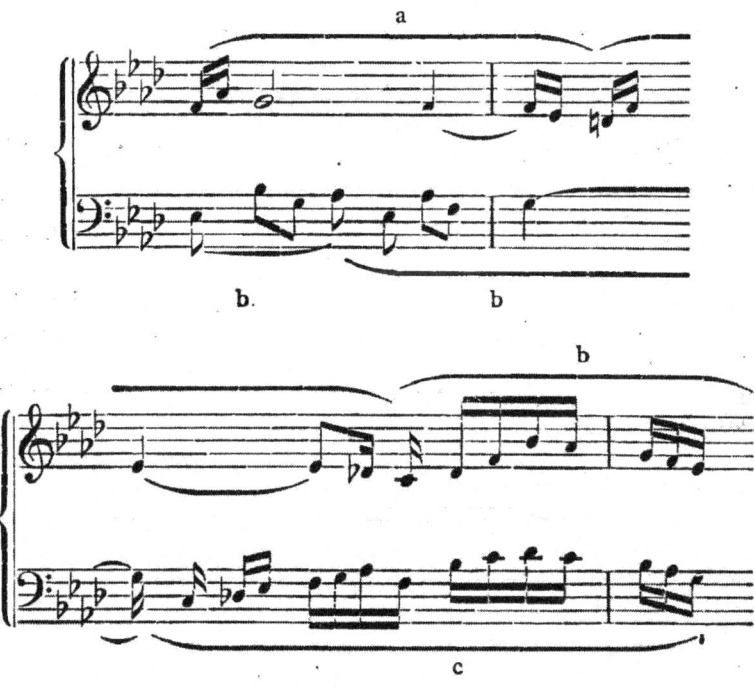

If the motive material of the whole fugue be compared with this first period of 8 measures, it will be seen that nothing new is afterwards introduced. But how

wonderfully does Bach make varied use of the motives here
marked off by slurs, now spreading them out in form of
sequence, now inverting them, or advancing them one
crotchet in the measure, or dividing them between two
voices, etc.! The syncopated motive assumes great importance, first in the episodes, but finally, also, as counterpoint to the theme; *c* is really the only repetition at all faithful of the first countersubject (but without theme entry). The
theme as at *b* is frequently employed in the interludes, but as
a real theme it appears no fewer than fourteen times, and,
later on, in a form which does not exactly correspond
either with Dux or Comes (it has the opening skip of
the fourth of the Comes, followed by the third of the
Dux):

The first section extends until after the second entry
of the tenor, which forms a confirmation of the close in
A♭-*major* marked by a shake, at the end of the second
period of eight measures. Instead of making the four
voices enter in direct succession (in four times four
measures), according to school rule, Bach here (and often
elsewhere) prefers to separate the second from the third
voice entry by an interlude of four measures; and after
the fourth entry he has here likewise an interlude, during
which the tenor is silent, of four measures. But it
becomes impossible to look upon these interludes as independent real "between" members in the period structure,
as is possible in many fugues; this indeed is, generally,
possible: here they appear rather as completing the symmetry of the theme entries. In the present case, by the
tenor voice ceasing and reentering, the fugue seems as
if it were in five voices.

The second (modulating middle) section first leads by
means of a three-voice episode to a half close in *F-minor*
(c^7); the alto then introduces the Dux in *F-minor* (parallel
key) and with four free measures (5 a—6 a, 7—8) the
period draws to a close in *F-minor*. A second period
of this section changes ^0c in f^7 (1st to 2nd measure),
then, as a more expressive repetition of the first group

(1 a—2 a), introduces the Dux in *B♭-minor* (tenor), and closes the fore-section with the answering Comes in the alto; the after-section (closing in *B♭-minor*) forms an episode from the materials of preceding episodes (soprano developing motive *b*, alto: motive *c*, and tenor: motive *a*). The four measures which now join on with an apparent stretto of the theme between alto and soprano and a close on the dominant (*E♭-major*) ought, properly speaking, to be regarded as an intermediate member, as a return to the principal key, as a transition to the third (closing) section.

This closing section itself begins with a theme entry in the alto (Dux in *E♭-major*, but of wider compass) and a second (*Dux in A♭-major*) in the soprano, formed in a similar manner; and in well-known fashion, by touching the Mixolydian seventh (*g♭*) and leading to the under-dominant, it indicates the approaching end:

The alto introduces, besides, an apparent stretto; the after-section makes a half close on the dominant (*e♭⁷*). The second period of the concluding section introduces next a complete development, viz. in the bass: Dux in *A♭-major*; in the tenor: Comes from *F-minor* to *C-minor*; in the alto: Comes from *D♭-major* to *A♭-major*; and in the soprano: Comes from *B♭-minor* to *D♭-major*: —

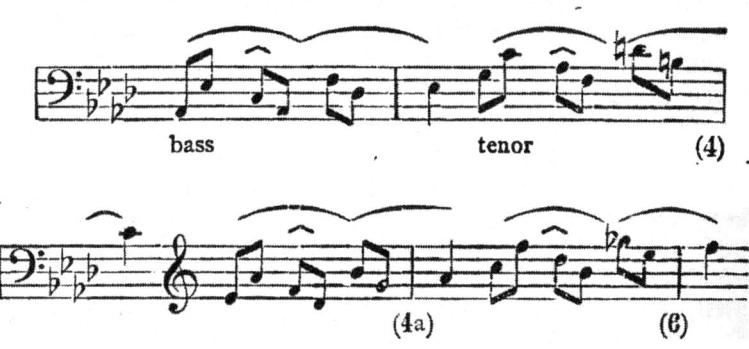

The turning towards *D♭-major* is twice imitated in con-junct upward movement ($a♭^7$—$d♭^+$; $b♭^7$—$e♭^+$ and c^1—^0c), whereby the first group of the after-section appears considerably strengthened (5 a—6 a), and then comes a close in full, broad manner with a triplet of measures (3 measures in place of 7—8). But as the bass and alto move to f (the ordinary deceptive cadence), instead of $a♭$, another repetition of the after-section becomes necessary, affording an opportunity of introducing the Dux once more in its original form, after which there is a broad supplementary close.

I cannot see in what way this fugue shows imperfection. It certainly is neither so sombre as the fugues in *C♯minor* and *E♭-minor*, nor as energetic as the fugues in *D-major* and *E-major*, but, on the other hand, it is exactly an *A♭-major* fugue. Schumann has taught us what an *A♭-major* man is (Chopin — the sensitive dreamer).

I. 18.

PRELUDE AND FUGUE IN G♯-MINOR.

C♯-minor and *G♯-minor* are keys in near relation-ship, the one to the other. Both metaphysically, transcendentally, have something in common, *i. e.* are far removed from the sober views of every day life, and move in a sphere of supersensual presentations and ideal feelings. Did Bach himself notice that the theme of the *C♯-minor* Prelude has once again displayed its inexhaustible, impulsive power in the *G♯-minor* prelude? Let us compare:

Andante espressivo.

dolce.

(4=6)   (8)

and:

also

here:

there: etc.

The mood is quite the same, the expression somewhat softer here than there, the whole structure somewhat more delicate, more polyphonic, while the melodic element exercises stronger power over the chord-like basis. The theme is also introduced in inversion. The construction of the prelude, noting its principal points, appears thus:

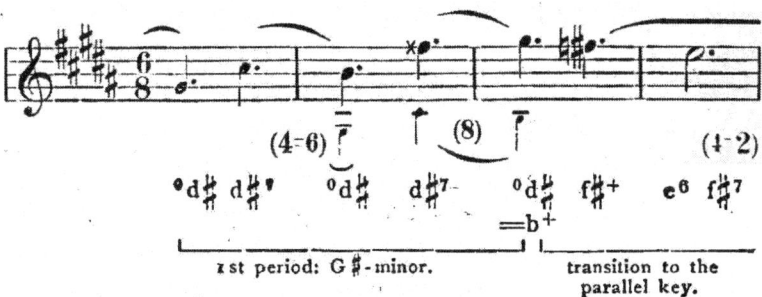

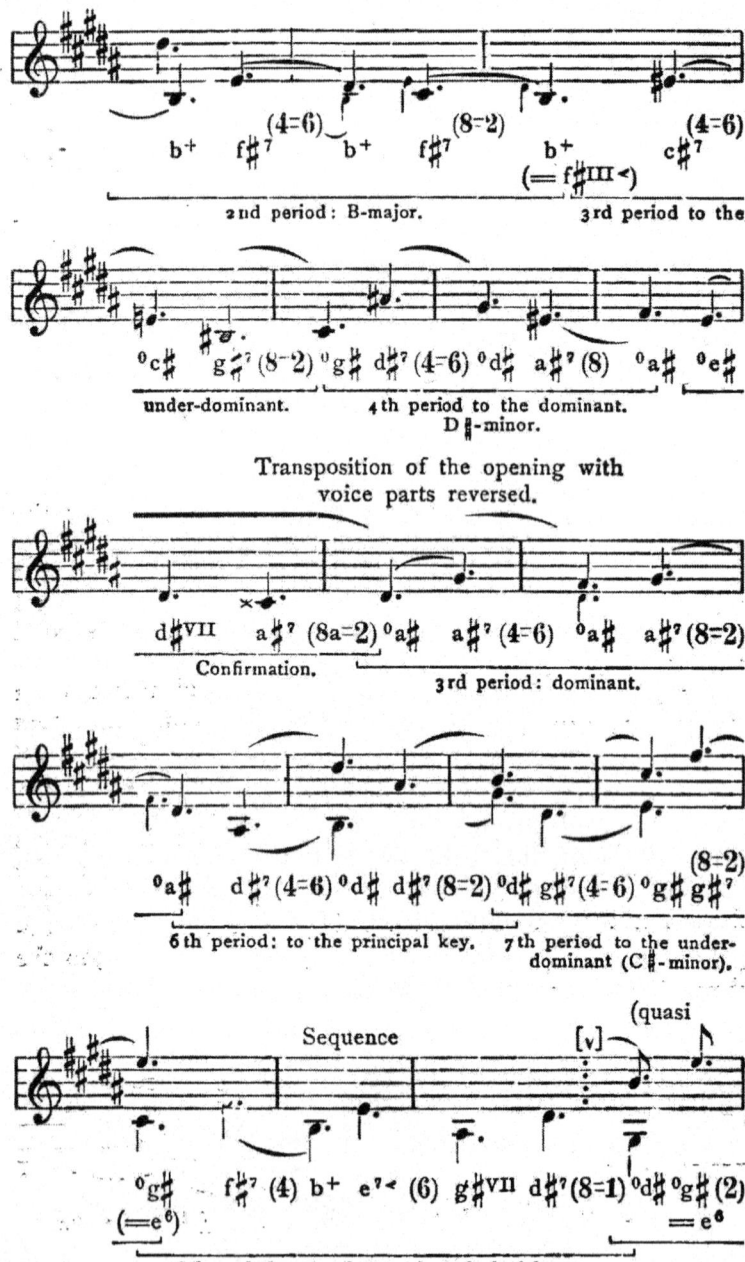

2nd period: B-major.   3rd period to the

under-dominant.   4th period to the dominant.
D♯-minor.

Transposition of the opening with
voice parts reversed.

Confirmation.   3rd period: dominant.

6th period: to the principal key.   7th period to the under-
dominant (C♯-minor).

Sequence   [v]   (quasi

8th period: returning to the principal key.

Riemann, Analysis of Bach's "Wohltemperirtes Clavier".   8

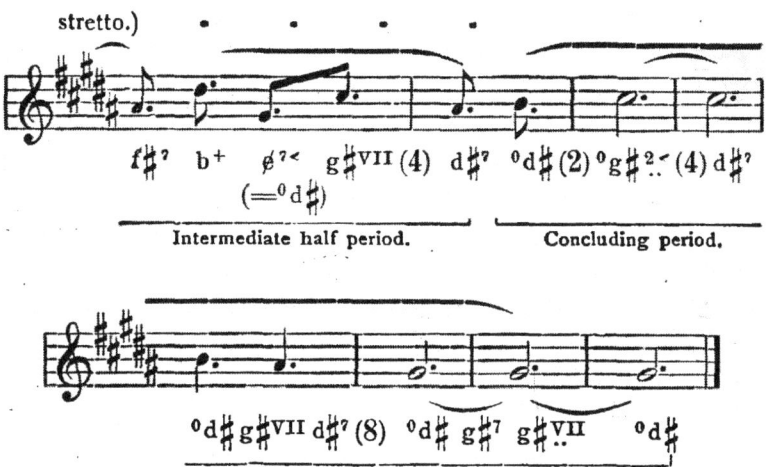

Intermediate half period.   Concluding period.

The fugue (à 4) is one of the most expressive of the whole work, so impregnated is it with subjective feeling, and developed in so pleasing and natural a manner that nowhere is there a trace of fugue fetters (in this respect I might compare it to the *F-minor* fugue of the second book).

Marx is right in insisting that the character of a fugue is essentially established from the commencement by the voice position with which it opens. In the present case the theme is first given out by the tenor, *i. e.* the fugue begins in a low middle position. The character of the melody of the theme is an unusual one; it advances in slightly curved line from the fundamental note to the third, and rises further (by means of a tritone!) to the fifth, but from thence (in the key of the dominant) descends, by wide steps and with repetition of notes, to the lower octave of the dominant.

Andantino un poco larghetto.

It should be carefully noticed here that by its appended motives, the first half of the theme receives a certain philosophical repose and precision, the simple reason of which is, that both the upward steps occur in these appended motives. In order rightly to grasp the theme, one ought to think over, and thoroughly realise the effect of the two following false readings,

the first of which is rendered impossible by the continuation (which cannot be properly rounded off), but the second, by Bach's harmonisation of the theme (cf. the soprano entry). What a striking equilibrium, on the one hand, between the pressing onward of the harmony and the counterbalancing holding-back on the opening accented beat, and on the other hand, between the upward striving melody and the backward-turned movement of the harmony! First of all the harmony advances from tonic to dominant, $(g\sharp—f^{\times})$ but the appended motive returns to the tonic: the melody however selects just this backward step to advance to the third $(g\sharp—a\sharp—b)$; then the harmony advances $(a\sharp—g\sharp)$ to the key of the dominant by change of $^0d\sharp$ to $d\sharp^{VII}$, and the appended motive completes the close from the new under-dominant, through the upper-dominant $(a\sharp^7)$, to the tonic, and again the melody makes use of this cadential moment to ascend $(c^{\times}—d\sharp)$. But the concluding member of the theme rejoices over the victory which it has won in a quietly descending cadence, to which a certain humour (in the noblest sense of the word) is not lacking. I can discover nothing in this fugue of the „repentance-aria-mood" ("Buss-Arien-Stimmung" mentioned by Jadassohn).

The answer, with exception of the opening note, is in the under-, instead of the upper-fifth: the reason for which is that the theme itself modulates to the key of the upper-dominant and concludes in it, so that the modulation back to the principal key falls to the Comes. One could only be in doubt as to whether a greater portion of the first part of the Comes could not have been answered in the fifth, thus:

Although the second Variante preserves the characteristic interval of the tritone which is lacking to the first, yet it would be less possible: the $\natural\sharp c$ would be quite unsuitable, for over against the higher xc of the first motive it would excite a downward tendency quite alien to the first half of the theme. But evidently Bach penetrated deeper below the surface, when he sought to get to the under-dominant as soon as possible in order to allow the answer to rise from it to the principal key in a manner similar to that in which the Dux rises from the principal key to the dominant: —

Finally, nothing could be urged against the answer in the fourth of the first note, if it made easier the order of modulation; but the contrary would be the case, and it would mean the loss of a powerful means of expression, viz. the decisive turning away from the key of the upper-dominant to that of the under-dominant which is displayed in the melody by the step of a third in place of that of a second (cf. the *F-minor* fugue, in which a contrary cause has led to a similar result).

The counterpoint throughout is simple: there are no complicated combinations, but where the natural evolution leads to something of the kind (prolongation, inversion of the theme), Bach hints at the possibility of such devices (cf. the middle of the second development, in which the soprano indicates prolongation; of the inversion of the opening motive rich use is made in the episodes.)

The countersubject preserves throughout the character of the theme, nestles closely to it in such a manner, that one might feel tempted to deny that it had any independent, countersubject character. But if the countersubject be taken, not in its quality of counterpoint to the Comes, but rather as an immediate, further development of the opening voice, after the enunciation of the Dux, then it is evident, that it brings the theme to full completion, in that it rises again from the lower octave of the dominant up to the third of the tonic, and again settles firmly down on the fundamental note. It therefore works out the second motive of the theme, and, at the end, conforms to the *staccato*-character of the theme. But the syncopation of its opening motive is a genuine addition to the motive material:

Also the immediate continuation of the tenor voice (the second countersubject) receives manifold treatment in the course of the fugue. In this passage an almost obstinate clinging to the fundamental key (*g♯*), despite the modulation, forms a characteristic feature: —

Its smooth crotchets introduce more repose into the piece, and the syncopation at the end gives opportunity for syncopation on an extended scale in several of the episodes. Of possible combinations of the theme and of its two chief counterpoints, the following are employed: —

1) Soprano: Theme (Dux)   in the exposition
   Alto: 1st Counterpoint   (3rd voice entry)
   Tenor: 2nd Counterpoint

2) Soprano: 1st Counterpoint   at the beginning of
   Alto: 2nd Counterpoint   the 2nd development
   Tenor: Theme (Comes)

3) Soprano: 2nd Counterpoint
   Alto: 1st Counterpoint
   Tenor: free filling-up voice   2nd development
   Bass: Theme (Dux)

4)   Alto: Theme (Comes)
   Tenor: 1st Counterpoint   = 1.
   Bass: 2nd Counterpoint

5) Soprano: 2nd Counterpoint
   Alto: 1st Counterpoint
   Tenor: Theme   = 3.
   Bass: free filling-up voice

The general construction is as follows: — Ist section (in the principal key): the entry of the four voices, without break, in the following order: tenor, alto, soprano, bass, alternating regularly with Dux and Comes; after an episode of four measures, modulating to the dominant, follows a second development, likewise in the key of the tonic, only in it an episode of four measures is inserted between each of the voice entries: the tenor opens with the Comes (the tenor also opened the first development but with the Dux), the bass follows with the Comes (but beginning with $c\sharp$, therefore standing entirely in the fourth); then the tenor returns (in this fugue it assumes the *rôle* of leading voice), but with the Dux as at first, and lastly comes the alto with the original Comes (the second working out begins à 3 — with pausing bass, and ends in like manner — with pausing soprano).

The (modulating) middle section is particularly terse (only two theme entries): it has first, an episode of 8 measures (characteristically coloured by the frequent introduction of the tritone springing from the theme), modulating to the key of the dominant, on whose dominant (a♯⁺) it closes. The soprano (changing the meaning of the 8th measure to that of 1st) enters with the Dux in *D♯-minor*, whereupon the bass follows with the Comes in *B-major* (under-dominant). A further episode of 8 measures leads back to *G♯-minor*.

III. The concluding section next introduces the Dux in the tenor (!), and, after threefold emphatic repetition of the second group (measures 3—4), the Comes in the after-section in the soprano (without d♯). Four measures of close-confirmation bring the fugue to an end.

The episodes of the first and concluding sections are developed from the second half of the theme, and close repeatedly with a chord - like passage for three voices. Those of the middle section show more independence in motive treatment, and are somewhat more agitated, but yet their chief motive appears allied to the theme.

I. 19.

PRELUDE AND FUGUE IN A.

A fresh healthy life pulsates both in the prelude and in the fugue. Only he, who cannot see the wood for the trees, will complain of school dust in them. The prelude strictly in three voices, deals with double counterpoint in the octave in a light and graceful manner of which, surely, only the master possessed the secret. The thematic material of the first period (beginning with the second [accented] group, *i. e.* without 1st and 2nd measures) returns, in the course of the piece, no fewer than five times, with four different combinations of voices:

1. Allegro deciso.

(2 in E-major = 5 in A-major.)
(4 in F♯-minor = 1 in A-major.)

The second follows immediately after the first (with elision of the first group); between the 2nd and 3rd is inserted a free half period in which the under voice continues the running semiquaver figure of *a* (see above), while the two other voices introduce the syncopated motive *b* contracted, and with third-doubling; and between 3rd and 4th there is only an improved close of two measures (7a—8a).

The episode which unfolds itself between the 4th and 5th has a scale progression of semiquavers divided between the two under voices, while the upper voice remains firm to the syncopated motive; the half close of the 4th measure (on *e*+) is turned into an added group (3a—4a) shaping itself into a full-close, which however is prevented by the entry of combination 5 (4a = 3). The 6th follows immediately on the 5th, and lastly come two close-confirmations each of two measures: first, with the upper voice and lower voice in contrary motion, and in semiquavers (motive *a*), and finally with a quiet cadence and with addition of 3rd voice.

The order of keys is the normal one

1st Section: principal key (1) — dominant (2) — principal key (3) leading to

2nd Section: parallel (4), then leading home to

3rd Section: principal key (5—6).

The elision of the first group (1st and 2nd measures) which is found throughout the piece, gives rhythmical interest to the many changes of meaning which necessarily result therefrom. The strict adherence to the thematic material of the first measures produces neither a formal nor monotonous effect, because the interchanging of voices and key-contrasts always offers points of interest. It ·may be further remarked that the rests of the middle voice (*b*) at the beginning (I) are filled up in all later entries of the theme, not always in the same manner, but each one according to the preceding motive formation of the voice in question.

Voice *c* only shows its true form at the second theme entry:

i. e. the octave leap at the commencement is not an essential part of it, and the bass cadence of the last measure (of the piece) where it occurs in the bass, (I. 4) is only levied from it.

As the prelude, if it is to produce its full effect, must not be taken too slowly (the semiquaver figuration is flowing and easy to be understood), so the rendering of the fugue must necessarily be a very quiet and expressive one, if it is not to become — according to the description of Debrois van Bruyck "an interesting mosaic" ("interessantes Kombinationsspiel"), "somewhat monotonous as to rhythm" ("rhythmisch ein wenig monoton"), "as if it were designed for a figured-bass exercise" ("als ob es auf eine Generalbassübung abgesehen wäre"). Yes, indeed if nothing else can be discovered in the theme except rising fourths and falling thirds, then it does move up and down in bass fashion, and the continued quaver movement of the first half of the fugue may seem "somewhat monotonous".

But, in truth, this number is full of heartfelt feeling, and of almost touching naiveté — if only the rhythmical nature of the theme and the feminine endings of its several motives be properly recognized and understood:

Poco lento, con molto espressivo.

How simple, how charming is this double putting forward of the tonic: the first quite plain, the second preced-
ed by leading note and third (likewise the "overhanging
6th") and veering towards dominant; and how gently,
amiably does the theme stretch out towards the fifth, and
indeed to the octave, finally sinking submissively down to
the third. The striking of the upper octave must not be
confused with a pressing upwards towards it: the melodic
annexations to the theme extend, on the whole, only to
the sixth, *i. e.* remain quietly in one and the same tone-
region, and occupy a compass recognized by us as normal
(cf. I. 11).

The elision of the unaccented beat of the first measure
of each group constitutes a rhythmical peculiarity of the
theme, *i. e.* the continued order in triple form — accented
— unaccented — accented:

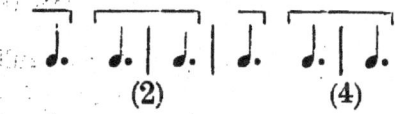

which runs nearly through the whole fugue. That the plain
$^9/_8$ time of the original notation does not show this clearly
without explanation may be granted, especially as the few
departures from this mode of structure render its recognition
more difficult. A further hindrance to the immediate under-
standing of the piece is the circumstance that the second voice
entry does not wait until the first has ended, but at once forms
a stretto (the alto begins at the third measure). Again, according to school rule, the theme would only extend to the second *a,* and the rest be considered counterpoint to the
Comes. But this is in contradiction with all the theme
entries which follow; also the theme, on which Bach built
this long fugue, would be one altogether too insignificant!
But the strongest point in our favour is that during the
first half of the fugue, characteristic counter-motives do not
appear; the entry of the real countersubject marks indeed

the chief point of the second (middle) section of the fugue (re-establishment of the principal key); and it renders possible the unusually long spinning out of the fugue.

The answer of the theme corresponds entirely to the principles recognized as binding in our previous analyses. The Dux remains in the principal key: the Comes has therefore to modulate to the dominant; the Dux at the commencement emphasizes twice the fundamental note of the key, and therefore the Comes must twice emphasize the fifth, but not in the harmony, or even key of the dominant, but in the harmony of the tonic. Hence the enlargement of the first interval (3rd in place of 2nd), and the contraction of the third (2nd in place of 3rd); the rest is a faithful transposition in the fifth: —

The interweaving of Dux and Comes brings about the change of meaning, in the after-section, of the 4th measure to that of 2nd (6). The continuation of the first voice is not, as already said, a real countersubject, but it remains in the character of the theme:

The third voice (under-voice, tenor) only enters when Comes has ended, and with elision of the unaccented beat (without up-beat ♪). At the conclusion of the theme it springs downwards, and by giving out the Comes, seems to be a fourth voice (bass). An appended measure $^9/_8$ (triplet) changes the half-close on e^7 into a full-close in *A-major*, which is, however, frustrated by the re-entry of the Dux in the soprano (as at first). Here ends the exposition; this new theme entry belongs to the second development, and also, already, to the second (modulating middle) section of the fugue. An episode of equal length follows (with triplet from the seventh to the eighth measure), modulating from *A-major* to *F♯-minor*. At the close the bass introduces the theme in *F♯-minor* (8th = 1st measure), with somewhat free ending, viz. an extension (triplet) turning from *F♯-minor* to *B-minor*; this close is confirmed (*3a—4a*), but frustrated by a very free theme entry in the bass, which changes $^0f♯$ to d^6, and advances through *A-major* to *E-major*, first making a half-close in it, and then, in the repeated after-section, a full-close. Also here there is again a triplet of counts, *i. e.* one measure of $^9/_8$ instead of $^6/_8$. An episode immediately following resumes the triplet formation, continues it through three measures (triplet in place of *7a—8a*), and tends towards the principal key. And now we have reached an important turning point (the heart of the middle section of the fugue). For against the Dux in the bass appears a counter-subject, with running semiquavers, in the alto, introducing quite a new element, though not endangering the unity of effect; the smooth counterpoint nestles, indeed, closely to the theme:

The section opens with two voices (the under one taking Dux, the upper one, the countersubject); then, when the middle voice follows with the Comes, the upper voice attempts the countersubject, but gives it up, and all three voices proceed once more in quavers, as in the first section, with a triplet (a $^9/_8$ M.) as close. The middle voice once more takes up the theme in the same position,

not as Comes, but as Dux (in the key of the dominant);
again at the close there is a triplet, which here leads to
a long episode in $^9/_8$ measure. This episode is developed
from the quaver motive of the theme, and the semiquaver
motive of the countersubject, and leads to a theme entry
in the under-dominant (*D-major*); it adheres to $^9/_8$ measure, but in form it is very free, and it passes to
B-minor (parallel of the under-dominant). In place of
the $^9/_8$ measure $^6/_8$ measure reappears, with elision of the
light beat of the first measure (𝅘𝅥𝅮.¹ 𝅘𝅥𝅮. | 𝅘𝅥𝅮. |), tending
back, at the same time, to the quieter character of the
first section; for there can be no doubt that in the
structure — ⌣ — dwells great repose: the first accented
beat is the starting point, the point of support, the second,
the end point, point of rest. *i. e.* we have in this formation continued small members, which are easily intelligible,
and which produce a calming effect, not one of rushing
on, but one of holding back. There are no more entries
of the theme, but the motive play of the whole fugue
makes it sound as if the theme were continually present
(a stretto-effect).

The modulation passes through *A-major* (^{0}f$\sharp$ = d^6)
and *E-major* (a$^+$ = a^6), to *F$\sharp$-minor* (b^7 = f$\sharp$III$^<$), which
is established in great detail (7, 7a, 7b, 8, 7a—8a). Here-
with concludes the widely developed second (modulating
middle) section of the fugue, and, indeed without definite
return, for after the *unisono*-close of all three voices on
f$\sharp$, the middle voice continues with the Dux, as if it had
arrived at *a*:

i. e. *F$\sharp$-minor* changes, without further ado, into *A-major*.
A simple transition from *F$\sharp$-minor* (by change of meaning
of the close to a new commencement [8a = 1]) leads
back to *A-major*; at the same time the countersubject
disappears from the scene, and the three voices move
again, after the manner of the first section, in quiet
quavers (with crotchets interspersed). After the regular

close of the Dux, the bass follows with the Comes, so
that, at the eighth measure comes the dominant (half-close)
and a new after-section becomes necessary, which in a
broad manner — preparing the final close — changes the
half- into a full-close. Again there is a triplet, which
rightly — and for the last time — leads to $^9/_8$ measure,
in which occur three successive close-confirmations. The
whole work is rounded off in an imposing manner, and
unity of the piece is marked by the reappearance of the
countersubject in this Coda (which should be taken in
quiet *tempo*), which faithfully forms a last escort to the
theme motives which nowhere constitute a real theme
entry.

I. 20.

PRELUDE AND FUGUE IN A-MINOR.

Both pieces in A-*minor* are, certainly, somewhat
colourless, but are not, on that account, of less value
than the other numbers of the work. It is not only the
key which produces this effect, which indeed does not
extend beyond the surface; the nature of the themes
(answering most certainly to the general character of the
key) is one which would produce no essentially different
result if a transposition were effected into A♭-*minor*, or
G♯-*minor*: they lack not only rhythmical energy, but
harmonic depth or melodic polish. It is a light trifling,
a pleasant see-saw movement, rather than a passionate
struggle, or trembling terror. This is still more perceptible
in the prelude than in the fugue: the theme of the former
presses upward, it is true, from the fifth of the key (*e*)
gradually to the octave, not with firm melodic continuity,
but rather with an up and down chord movement as
though it had no stability — a prey to the lightest
breath of air: —

Allegro poco mosso.

The construction is the simplest imaginable. The thematic little period of four measures commences and concludes in A-minor; it is repeated in the after-section, and in the key of the minor upper-dominant (*E-minor*), a change which has been brought about by the single $d\sharp$; but the voices are reversed, and the accented beats (beginnings of the bars) are emphasised by full chords. The fore-section of the second period has the same motives, but falling instead of rising: it passes through ${}^0b$ ($= d^{\text{III}\,<}$ chord of the Doric sixth) $- a^7 - {}^0a$ ($= f^\text{o}$) $- g^7$ to *C-major*, in which key it makes a half close, whereupon the after-section introduces the theme in *C-major*, not rising, however, from the fundamental note to the fundamental note, but from the third to its octave. Besides, Bach freshens up interest by another means, viz. the introduction of a third (middle) voice. The leading back which follows is still in three voices ($c^{3\,>}$ $[= g^\text{VII}]$ $- d^7 - {}^0d - d^\text{VII} - a^7 - {}^0a$); the fourth measure changes meaning and becomes a second, while the new fourth already closes in the principal key to which the after-section now adheres. A three-part coda of two measures on an organ-point turns once more to the under-dominant (*D-minor*) and concludes with *A-major* instead of *A-minor*. It should be noticed that the theme in the third period no longer rises, but remains stationary, first on *d*, then on *a*.

The fugue (à 4) is one of the longest in the work, and rich in contrapuntal devices. The theme consists of a shortened (by elision of the first and fifth measures) period (order: — ◡ —). Its relationship to the theme of the prelude is self-evident: like the latter it rises gradually from the fundamental tone of the key, not, however, to the octave, but only to the sixth (*f*); it then falls suddenly to the leading note, but rises once again to the fifth, and concludes on the fundamental note. It also shows the same aimless suspense, and the same lack

of rhythmical energy, the same harmonic simplicity, and
the same lack of melodic charm (that the prelude is so
much shorter than the fugue appears to me a merit rather
than a fault; I imagine therefore that both originated
simultaneously, or, at any rate, that the prelude was
written expressly for the fugue).

Allegro moderato.

As the theme does not modulate, the Comes has to
complete the modulation to the key of the dominant,
and this is, indeed, at once brought about in the first
motive; it begins with the fifth of the key (but with tonic
harmony meaning!), and the rest is a faithful transposition
in the fifth. The fugue has no real countersubject, but
the diatonic motive which appears in the first counterpoint to the Comes plays the *rôle* of one: —

Much use is made likewise of a syncopated motive
in the first counterpoint:

but, as stated, there is no real countersubject faithfully accompanying the theme; and, indeed, it is not a necessity, for, as in other similar cases, the theme itself becomes counterpoint (in the strettos). The middle portion of the counterpoint is evidently derived from the theme, and, in part, anticipates the stretto-working:

(4)   (6)

In the first section of the fugue we have the exposition with its four regular voice entries (alto: Dux; soprano: Comes; bass: Dux; tenor: Comes), which, with exception of one insertion confirming the close before the bass entry, join on directly the one to the other. The great length of the theme is probably the reason of the restriction with regard to episodes. After only one measure confirming the close (e^+ instead of ^{0}b), the second development follows the first. This latter already belongs to the modulating middle section, and introduces the theme successively in all the four voices *in inversion*, first from *e* in the soprano (leading from *A-minor* to *G-major*), then from *g* in the tenor (through *C* to *D-minor*), further in the bass from *a* through a^{VII} to *C-major* and *F-major*, and finally in the alto from *f*, settling once again in *A-minor*. We have now penetrated to the core of the middle section, and a return to the principal key during that section is already familiar to us. The third development which now follows reproduces the theme in its right form, but in *strettos*, first in *A-minor* (Dux) between soprano and tenor, then in *E-minor* (Comes) between alto, bass and soprano, and finally in *A-minor* (Dux) between tenor and alto, all at the distance of 2 crotchets. The somewhat long episode modulating to the parallel key (*C-major*) is followed by the fourth development, in which there is first of all a stretto between soprano and bass (interval of 2 crotchets, the theme in *C-major*), at the end of which the second half of the theme is carried through all the 4 voices:

9*

8va bassa

etc.

then a stretto between alto and tenor (inversion of the
theme from *a*) passing through *D-minor* back to *C-major*
and one between bass and soprano (inversion from *d*, in
G-major), a fourth between soprano and alto (inversion
from *e*), and, finally, one, only half carried through, between
bass and tenor (inversion from *e* in *D-minor*). We now
arrive at the concluding section (re-establishment of the
principal key by emphasising its under-dominant side), in
which there is first a stretto of the theme (not in inversion) between bass and tenor from *d* and *a* (from *D-minor*
to *A-minor*), then, in soprano and alto, a stretto of the
inverted theme from *e* and *a* (from *A-minor* to *D-minor*),
further, in bass and alto, a stretto of the inverted theme
from *c* (through *F-major* to *G-minor*), then a three-fold
stretto (over long holding note *g* in bass) between tenor
(inverted theme from *g*), alto, (theme [not inverted]
from *a* on a[7] [*D-minor*], not completed) and soprano
(theme from *e* in D-minor), and still a stretto [not in-
verted] from *a* and *e* in A-minor (alto and soprano; in
these there are 2 triplet measures); and finally, over a
stationary bass (organ point on *a*) still a threefold stretto
between tenor (inverted theme from *a*), alto (ditto), and
soprano (theme from *d*) with $^3/_2$ instead of $^2/_2$ measure.
The number of voices in the strettos is increased, by the
free addition of filling up notes, to five and six. The
work concludes with some free, broad, and full measures.

I. 21.

PRELUDE AND FUGUE IN B♭.

Two fresh, healthy pieces without subtleties or mysti-
fications of any kind. If when compared with C, the key of
B flat is more satisfying, fuller than that of F (it is the
most distant key on the flat side which can only be
explained by fifth relationship), Bach has certainly intensified that effect, and in a marked manner, by the character
of the themes, which he selected for these pieces. The
prelude, has something of organ dignity about it: even of
the principal motive (commencement):

that can be said (the zig-zag movement of the bass part
leads one to the conclusion that it was thought out
pedaliter); but still more do the episodical running passages for one voice appear as if they were borrowed
from a Bach organ toccata:

etc.

and the second half of the piece with its full organ effects
may be quoted as a similar example:

In spite of the loose, almost phantastic character of the construction, it is easy to understand (the first section works up to the upper-dominant [F]; the second, with frequent allusion to the under-dominant, firmly reestablishes the key). We give the outline of the melody together with the harmonic scheme:

The fugue (à 3) is one of the most pleasing, most unpretending, most harmonious pieces of the Well-tempered Clavier. The climbing character of the voices is quite evident here, and hardnesses requiring special phrasing to make them sound euphonious do not occur. Also, in spite of the wide position of the three voices, the piece presents no technical difficulties, so that it must be reckoned among one of the first to be studied. The theme has a plagal character, *i. e.* its point of stress is first on the fifth of the key (*f*), whence it rises to the octave and to its third, first in quiet upward and downward gliding quaver movement, then pressing forward in a more lively manner in semiquavers, and finally remaining aloft with unbroken semiquaver movement (concluding with a feminine ending), a true garland of flowers:

Andantino un poco Allegretto (♩).

The theme occupies just four measures, and as Bach introduces the same in the voices without intermediate material, the even measure of the piece, justly noticed by Westphal, Spitta, etc. is the natural result (*i. e.* the symmetry, almost without disturbance of any kind, of the construction). The answer only differs at the commencement from the transposition in the fifth, and, indeed, again for the reason that it has to make the modulation to the key of the dominant, and not to enter with the harmony of the dominant (which can only take place when the Dux has already made the modulation):

Instead of *one* countersubject carried right through, we here have two, strictly adhered to throughout the fugue. The first (at the entry of the Comes in the alto) is as follows: —

and only in the upbeat at the commencement suffers
several changes of small moment. The second countersubject (at the entry of the Dux in the bass) has a semiquaver motive to the first half of the theme, and accompanies its second half with sixths:

The first development is redundant, for after the bass
there is still an entry of the theme in the soprano, and
indeed of the Comes (higher than the Dux at the opening,
and therefore intensifying the effect). It must really be
considered as belonging to the exposition (an apparent
fourth voice), for hitherto there has not been a single
episode. For the rest, all the episodes are formed by the
spinning out of the "climbing" figuration of the second
half of the theme; the first, indeed, in its first half, by
a rosalia-like shifting of the closing group from *F-major*
to *G-minor*, by which modulation to the parallel key is
effected; this key is mantained through three episodical
measures (soprano pushing on the motive of the second
half of the theme; the bass, playing with the inversion of

the first half of the theme) coming to a half close on d^{1}.
The alto now introduces the theme (Dux) in *G-minor*
(parallel key), faithfully supported by the two countersubjects, which gradually pass through nearly all transformations, and then follows the bass with the Comes in
C-minor (parallel of the under-dominant). After an episode
of five measures (with 8 = 1) enters again the alto with the
first half of the theme from *c* (*c e♭ c g b♭ a♭* etc.), and
(having the appearance of a stretto) the soprano with the
complete Dux in *E♭-major*, thus the alto can bring in
the Comes in that key (*e♭ g e♭ b♭ d c*) so as definitely
to restore the principal key (from *E♭*, closing in *B♭*).
Three close-confirmations, each of one measure, bring
the fugue to an end. In comparison with other fugues,
the small space (in all only seven measures) granted to
the principal key at the end attracts notice; the first
section, which, owing to the double entry of the Comes,
modulates twice to the dominant, fills sixteen measures.
The modulating middle section fills four and twenty; on
its way from the under-dominant of the parallel (C-minor)
to the under-dominant (E♭) it touches once, lightly, the
principal key; anyhow the tendency towards the under-
dominant side, during the whole of the second half of
the fugue, is evident.

———

I. 22.

PRELUDE AND FUGUE IN B♭-MINOR.

We now come to two of the most sublime
numbers of the work. The deep darkness of the key of
B♭-minor inspired the old master with ideas of holy
earnestness, and cast a sacred lustre over his tones, such
as is rarely to be met with in his writings. Perhaps in
both these pieces one ought to think of church, looking
especially on the prelude as a fervent prayer, a tormented
and dejected heart beseeching for the loving mercy of
the Almighty.

The many organ-points (nearly the whole piece is studded with them) hold the melody, as it were, with invisible bands, and the rising thirds of the principal motive with the repetition of note which follows, together with the feminine ending so full of expression, appear like a heartfelt request, like raised-beseeching hands:

The whole piece is evolved in an astonishing and masterly manner from the two motives,

the second of which always preserves its direction (falling suspension-resolution), whereas the first is worked out both in rising and falling form, also occasionally combined with its inversion. In the matter of expression this episode is of touching naïveté:

We give the harmonic analysis with only figures:

$$\overset{o}{}f \; \| \;\; .. \; b\flat \; \overset{\overset{\frown}{VI \quad VII}}{VIII \quad IX<} \;\; .. \; \Big| \; f \; \overset{\overset{\frown}{II \quad III}}{IV \quad V} \;\; .. \; f \; \overset{\overset{\frown}{8 \quad 7}}{6> \quad 5} \;\; .. \; \Big|$$

$$\underset{\underbrace{}}{V} \qquad\qquad (2) \qquad\qquad \underset{V}{\underbrace{}} \qquad\qquad (4)$$

$$\underset{V}{\underset{\frown}{f}} \; \overset{\overset{\frown}{II \quad III}}{VII> \quad VIII} \;\; .. \; f\widehat{VII}\natural \;\; b\flat\,VII \;\; .. \; \Big| \; f^7 \;\; {}^of \;\; b\flat\,VII \;\; .. \; \Big| \qquad (8\text{-}4)$$

$$f^7 \;\; .. \; \Big| \; .. \;\; .. \; \Big| \;\; .. \;\; {}^of \; \| \; \overset{\frown}{VI} \;\; (=d\flat{}^6) \; \Big| \; e\flat{}^7 \;\; a\flat{+} \qquad (8) \; \underset{\underbrace{}}{V} \;\; \underset{V}{} \qquad (2)$$

$${}^oc \; \overset{\frown}{VI} \; \overset{\frown}{VII}\natural \; fVII \; c^7 \; \Big| \; \overset{\frown}{c^7} \; {}^oc \;\; .. \; f \; \overset{\overset{\frown}{VI \quad VII}}{} \;\; .. \; \Big| \; c^7 \; {}^oc \qquad (4)$$

$$fVII \; c^7 \; \Big| \; {}^oc \; \overset{2>}{{}^of} \;\; .. \; \Big| \; c^7 \; {}^oc \; fVII \; c^7 \; \Big| \; {}^oc \; \| \qquad (8) \quad \underset{\underbrace{}}{V} \quad \underset{V}{} \qquad\qquad (8a)$$

$$.. (= e\flat^{VII})b\flat^7 \Big| {}^ob\flat \; .. \; (=g\flat{}^6) \, a\flat^7 \Big| d\flat{+} \;\; .. \; g\flat{}^6 \;\; .. \; (=b\flat^{VI}) \Big| \qquad (2) \qquad\qquad (4)$$

$$b\flat\widehat{VII} \; f^7 \;\; .. \; b\flat^7 \Big| {}^ob\flat \; \underset{..}{VII} \; \underset{..}{IX}< \; {}^of \Big| b\flat\,VII \;\; .. \; f^7 \;\; .. \Big| {}^of \; \| \qquad (8\text{=}6) \qquad (6a) \qquad (8)$$

$$.. \; b\flat\,VII \; \Big| \; f?^7 \;\; .. \; \Big| \; \overset{\overset{\frown}{VI< \quad VII}\natural}{f\,VIII \quad IX<} \;\; .. \; \overset{\frown}{c^7} \; f{+} \;\; .. \; \Big|$$

$$(4) \quad \underset{1}{\underbrace{}} \qquad\qquad \underset{1}{\underbrace{}} \qquad (4)$$

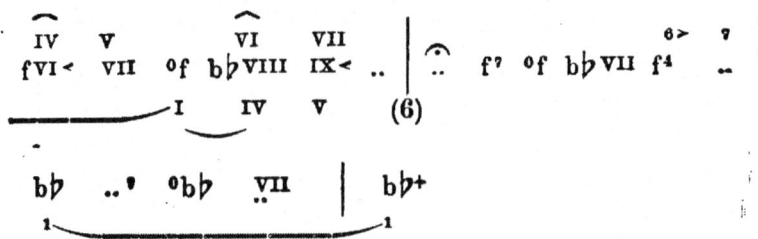

The fugue (à 5) bears the same earnest stamp, but treats measure and metre with greater freedom almost than any other piece in the "Well-tempered Clavier" (and that is saying much). In my edition of the work I have attempted fully to expound the metrical contents; and this has resulted in a frequent change from $^4/_2$ and $^3/_2$ to $^3/_1$ measure, which last finally prevails. As in the *C-minor* fugue (I. 2.) $^3/_2$ measure appears twice in episode; $^3/_1$ measure arises through enrichment of the theme. If we consider as beyond dispute the fact that the situation of a theme in a bar (its metrical nature) constitutes a special element of its essence, it follows that an intelligent interpreter will always seek for, and find its points of stress in the same place; this is especially true in the fugue under notice, of the first minim of the theme, which, without doubt, bears the stronger accent; and indeed in Bach's notation, with exception of two strettos, it always appears at the beginning of the measure in **C**-time, strictly maintained throughout. But also for certain close-formations, which signify special points of rest of the tone movement, we demand absolute definite metrical relationship (point of stress of an accented measure [4., 8]). Occasional effects resulting from conflicting demands must be thoroughly grasped if one wishes to have firm points of support in interpreting the piece.

The theme descends solemnly from the tonic to the dominant, then leaps upward as far as the upper sixth of the tonic, only to fall down from it to the third, and afterwards rise from the second to the fifth:

Andante sostenuto.

Still one may be in doubt, as to whether the appended (5) rising crotchet motive does not already belong to the countersubject, since the alto enters with the Comes under the $d\flat$ (4th measure). As the Dux remains in the principal key, the Comes must modulate from it (and indeed from the harmony of the tonic) to the key of the dominant. Therefore $b\flat$—f is answered not by f—c, but by f—$b\flat$, whereas the rest is a decided answer in the fifth:

This first answer includes, as we see, also the appended motive (5, 9); but already in the next entry (Dux in the tenor) we have in its place only a feminine ending, and, indeed, a further sinking from the third, to the fundamental note of the key;

and the fourth and fifth entries (1st and 2nd bass with Comes and Dux) evidently extend the measure to $^8/_1$ as they do not, like the first and second, keep the falling and rising crotchet motive within the same harmony, but change the harmony twice (tonic — dominant — tonic, likewise under-dominant (chord of the Doric sixth) — upper-dominant — tonic):

By repeating the two crotchet motives (one degree lower) there arises one single $^4/_2$ measure which modulates to *D♭-major*; the close-confirmation leading to the second development consists of a $^3/_1$ and of a $^4/_2$ measure.

The first voice entry (soprano) of the second development, *which, at the same time, forms the second (modulating section)* of the fugue, certainly introduces again the appended motive and thus keeps firmly to $^4/_2$ measure, but it cannot well be defined either as Dux or Comes, for at the opening it has the fourth-progression of the Dux, but also the tenth of the Comes (it modulates from *D♭-major* to *E♭-minor*):

The alto follows with the Comes in *E♭-minor*, with total suppression of the continuation of the theme beyond the 4th measure:

The three other theme entries (1st bass from *B♭-minor* to *E♭-minor*, 2nd bass from *E♭-minor* to *A♭-minor*, tenor from *A♭-major* to *D♭-major*) are again in $^3/_1$ measure, i. e. they have the extended and enriched form of the theme as in the 4th and 5th voice entries of the first development (between the last two there occurs one single measure of $^4/_2$).

The third *(concluding) section*, after an episode in $^3/_2$ measure formed from the first episode and leading back to the principal key, opens with a somewhat delayed entry of the Comes in the tenor:

At the close (4th measure), the second bass enters likewise with the Comes:

and now (at the 8th measure changed to meaning of 2nd) begin the strettos, first between soprano and alto at the distance of a minim:

and here it must be remarked, that in the case of such close strettos (one count) the imitation can be only a general one, for of necessity the metrical nature of the theme in the voice, which turns all the accented beats of the theme into unaccented ones, becomes completely disturbed. Next follows the tenor with the theme in its primitive form (with appended motive), yet at the opening can be defined neither as Dux nor Comes:

again a proof (of which especially in this fugue there are many) that the difference between Dux and **Comes** is only the occasional result of the modulatory considerations of the exposition, but not the special aim of fugue composition (not Dux and Comes, but theme and countersubject [or countersubjects] are the chief elements of fugue). Quite extraordinary is the simultaneous stretto of the theme in two voices (alto and tenor) and in $^3/_1$ measure which now follows:

(2)

An extended, and wonderfully fine episode brings us at the fourth measure (reckoning the $\circ$ as beats, real $^3/_1$ measure), first to a deceptive cadence in *B♭-minor* (f^{VII}) which, by an inserted measure (4*a*), is changed into a half close on f^7; while the after-section — which skips the fifth measure, and only gives a small up-beat to the sixth, so that a $^4/_2$ measure comes between — begins with a stretto, which probably has not its equal, of all five voices at the distance of a minim:

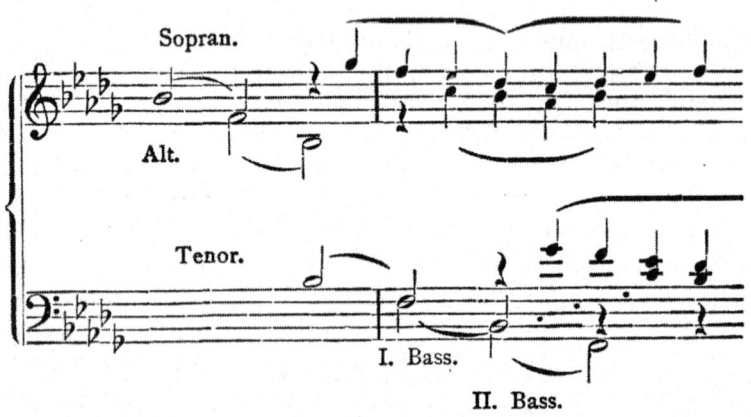

and then comes to a free conclusion.

We can only briefly allude to the countersubject, which indeed (as the theme is treated in a thoroughly free manner, and, quite contrary to Bach's usual custom, is harmonized in a variety of ways), is not consistently carried out, yet acquires great importance, especially in the episodes, (above all in the two in $^3/_2$ measure). Since, as already mentioned, the motive appended to the theme stretches on into the second voice entry, the contents of the countersubject really consist of only one single motive, namely the syncopated one (together with its inversion):

but this is already extended in the first episode ($^3/_2$ measure):

in which form it is kept until the third voice entry (still further enriched):

If all these three forms be considered identical, the countersubject may be traced pretty well throughout the whole fugue.

I. 23.

PRELUDE AND FUGUE IN B.

A glance at the pieces in *C♯*-, *F♯*- and *B-major*, (I, 3, I, 13, I, 23) shows that they are related to one another in a remarkably intimate manner; and on closer examination one is forced to the conclusion that this does not arise so much from the relationship of the three keys as from the relationship of the ideas prompted by the keys. All keys in proportion as they differ from the fundamental scales (*C-major* and *A-minor*) become more and more transcendental, more removed from plain every day life, and enter an ideal sphere of existence and feeling. Though we have already felt compelled to define the mood of the preludes in *C♯* and *F♯*, in the sense of a contemplation of nature resulting in enjoyment, still there is no contradiction here; it is just in beholding nature that an intelligent man renounces egoism in the fullest sense of the word and acquires the feeling of universal existence. Keys with flats, as opposed to those with sharps, are subjective, introspective — and so is minor, as opposed to major. Hence minor keys with many flats are the most reserved and, so to speak, the most philosophical (*F-minor*, *B♭-minor*, *E♭-minor*); major keys with many sharps, on

10*

the other hand, overflow with all-embracing love; they reveal
the happiness of a soul gazing with rapture on the harmony of the world.   Down to the most insignificant
semi-quaver there is nothing more fervent, more genuine
in feeling, more saturated with melody than this short
prelude in *B*. But the figuration must be minutely ar-
ticulated, and justice rendered to every note; if the
feminine endings are overlooked, especially those which
at the point of stress introduce a (♪) rest, the piece can
easily be ruined.   With what feeling of repose do the
opening bars already fill the soul

Andante espressivo.

and again, how nobly does the expression rise in intensity up to the last closing measures in which the three
voices are increased to four — and even five.

The piece consists of 4 periods of 8 measures, of
which the first, third and fourth have, at the close, the
triplet formation to be seen above at the syncopated
cadence. The first really concludes in the principal key,
but a close-confirmation turns to that of the dominant
(*F♯*), in which the second enters on the final note (8a=1);
this second period is similar to the first, repeats measures
3—4 in intensified form, and concludes in the parallel key
(*G♯-minor*). The third presents at first a somewhat lighter
appearance (as if it were an episode), but, with a repetition
of measures 3—4, returns to the serious mood (under-dominant, *E*), changes the meaning of measure 4*a* to that
of 6, and concludes with a triplet measure in the principal
key. The concluding period enters before the third has
ended, by changing the meaning of measure 8 to 2; it
turns in the fourth measure to the key of the under-

dominant (E), which however becomes itself quickly trans-formed to that of second upper-dominant ($e^{1<}=c\sharp^{9>}$ in $3a$—$4a$) and concludes, without further allusion to the under-dominant, with triplet measure for 6—8:

b^{+} $f\sharp^{7}$ b^{+} e^{6} $f\sharp^{7}$ (4) b^{+} $c\sharp^{7}$ $f\sharp^{+}$

[v]

b^{6} $c\sharp^{7}$ $f\sharp^{7}$ (8=6) b^{+} $^{6}_{..}$ $c\sharp^{7}$ $f\sharp^{+}$ b^{6} $c\sharp^{7}$ $\binom{8}{=1}$

(4a)

$f\sharp^{+}$ b^{6} $f\sharp^{+}$ b^{6} $g\sharp^{VII}$ (4) $d\sharp^{7}$ $^{o}d\sharp$ $g\sharp^{VII}$ $d\sharp^{7}$

$^{o}d\sharp$ $g\sharp^{VII}$ .. $d\overset{..}{\sharp}^{7}$ (8) $^{o}d\sharp$ .. (b^{6}) $c\sharp^{7}$

$^{o}c\sharp$ (a^{6}) b^{7} (4) e^{+} $f\sharp^{7}$ b^{7} $(4a=6)$ e^{6}

The fugue (à 4) certainly makes use of the device of inversion of the theme, but is, nevertheless, one of the more simple and easily understood numbers. The similarity of the themes of both fugue and prelude shows that they were not joined together by chance, or in a supplementary manner, but were planned the one for the other; the fugue, however, is of less value, and a little more conventional than the prelude. The theme, extending from under to upper fourth, moves in plagal position around the fundamental note of the key:

In the answer the departure from the usual rule is by no means self-evident; the custom which, indeed, Bach as a rule follows, requires, since the theme begins and ends with the tonic, the Comes to modulate to the dominant from the harmony of the tonic (with $f\sharp$, the first note, as 5 in b^+); Bach might then have written (in combination with the first counterpoint):

and this Comes and its counterpoint would have presented
no difficulties even for the fourth entry; thus the supposition that Bach restrained from this most regular form
on account of the continuation, is excluded.   Jadassohn's
supposition, that Bach was concerned about keeping the
step of the fifth with which the second motive joins on
to the first $(c\sharp—f\sharp, f\sharp—b)$, can with difficulty be maintained, and still less that Bach was especially anxious
about answering the fifth (fifth note of the theme) with the
octave (b); it was assuredly rather the harmonic progression
from the first to the second measure, which prompted Bach
to follow a different path:

The answer, appearing in normal form, as given on the
last page, has a change of harmony in one place which
is not in the corresponding part of the theme

This difference would be much stronger than the
trifling one in Bach's real Comes, namely of keeping the
up-beat and first point of stress in one harmony, while the
3 up-beat quavers of the Dux before the dominant of the
first point of stress $(c\sharp)$ establish a tonic. Bach's answer
is therefore on the whole more faithful, and this in spite
of some small departures from rule:

The *e* ♮, towards the end of the countersubject, which leads the modulation back to the principal key, enables the third entry of the theme to take place without episode. Thus the 4 voices (alto, tenor, soprano, bass) follow one another in immediate succession, and the first working out exactly fills the space of 2 8-measure periods and concludes in the key of the dominant. An episode of 4 measures, formed from motives of the theme and of the countersubject, leads back to the principal key, yet with a prolonged close (4a) to the under-dominant (*e*); but only to enable the tenor to take up the theme once again in B. After a free imitation of the first episode (in *G♯-minor* and *F♯*), and of its prolonged close, which this time leads back to the principal key, the alto introduces the theme in F♯: it is faithfully transposed in the 5th, and can therefore be taken either as Dux or Comes. At this point an incomplete second working-out comes to an end, which, according to previous experience, must be reckoned as belonging to the exposition section of the fugue. But now, something, extremely rare occurs: the expected modulating middle section is entirely omitted! By way of substitute the master indeed offers us two unlaboured inversions of the theme, and faithfully distinguished the one from the other as Dux and Comes:

Dux (soprano)

Comes (alto)

the latter forming a stretto with Dux in original form in the bass.

This third working out — of special interest in that it acts as middle section, but, as stated, altogether lacks modulation — concludes with the theme in the tenor, and indeed this theme entry commences in *E* (key of the under-dominant) and ends in *C♯-minor* (parallel of the under-dominant), thus making, finally, at least one more small digression, which, however one is accustomed to meet with near the close. After an episode of 6 measures (through *F♯-minor* [= a⁶] and *E-major* to *B-major*) there follows now in fact the concluding section, consisting of a theme entry in the alto (Dux) and one in the soprano (Comes), and of a two-measure close confirmation. In most of the theme entries in similar motion the countersubject is, as a rule, retained (occasionally divided between two voices). But even with the inversions its characteristic feature, the trailing scale passage, is to be found again in the counterpoint.

I. 24.

PRELUDE AND FUGUE IN B-MINOR.

In order that the earnest character of the concluding number of the first book might not be exposed to misconception, Bach himself indicated the tempo of both pieces: *Andante* for the prelude, and *Largo* for the fugue. The moving bass might, otherwise, tempt this or that player, to give an *Allegro* rendering of the prelude; and the exceptional length of the fugue exposes it to a similar danger, especially in the hands of the average player, who in slow performance might not perhaps succeed in euphonizing the difficulties of the work. It is to be hoped that the indications of phrasing and the present analysis will assist in securing honourable admiration for the work, and in silencing, once for all, blasphemies such as those uttered respecting it by van Bruyck.

The theme of the prelude, in the unvarnished manner in which it is presented in the first section of the same (up to the repeat), shows a strong relationship to the *Andante*-middle-section of the *E-flat* prelude (I. 7). Compare

with

But the same motives are also worked out in the second section, only in its first half they appear in diminution:

and in its second, somewhat extended

The sharply syncopated motive of the close also shows identity therewith

But how different the effect of the fourth-progressions here in the yearning key of *B-minor* as compared with that in the clear and firm key of *Eḃ-major*. Like raised beseeching hands they stretch the one over the other, while the bass, wandering quietly on, seems to represent inevitable fate, the even march of time. This mood explains why Bach almost intentionally avoids plain closes, for at a perfect cadence, by means of a feminine ending, he crosses over to a new order of progression, or follows the full close, by way of counterpart, with a half close (4*a*), or else avoids the tonic on the strongest beat. With exception of these insertions and changes of meaning, the metrical construction of the first part is indeed simple, and only at the end shows a measure of triplets; the second part, on the other hand, effects, for a long time, the elision of the first (unaccented) measure of each half period (1, 5), then introduces — evidently with transition to Allabreve-character — two great triplets (♩♩♩), and only again becomes simple towards the end.

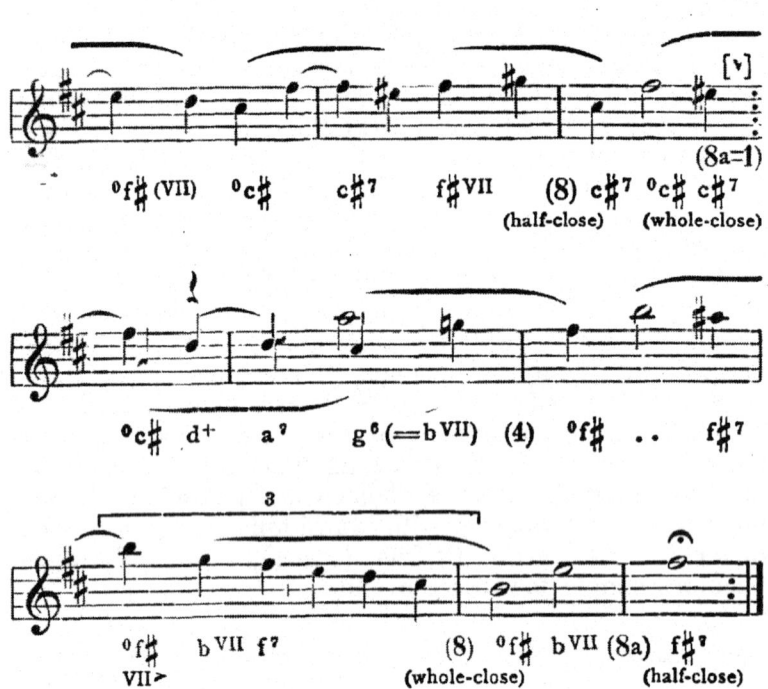

II middle section — ⌣ —.

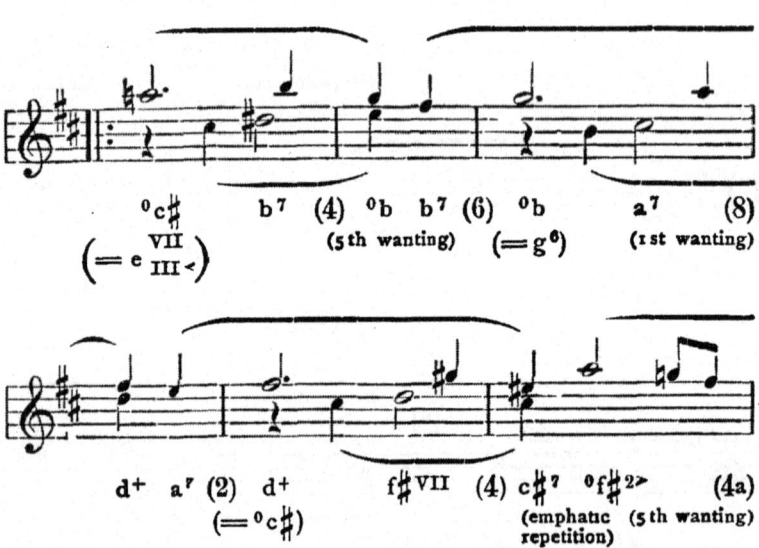

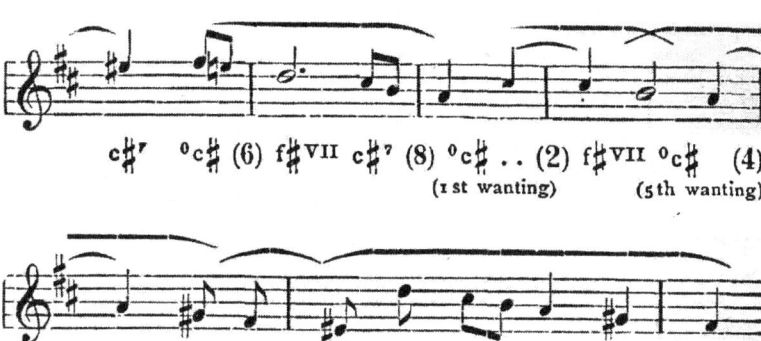

III section with gradual increase of movement, leading to Allabreve.

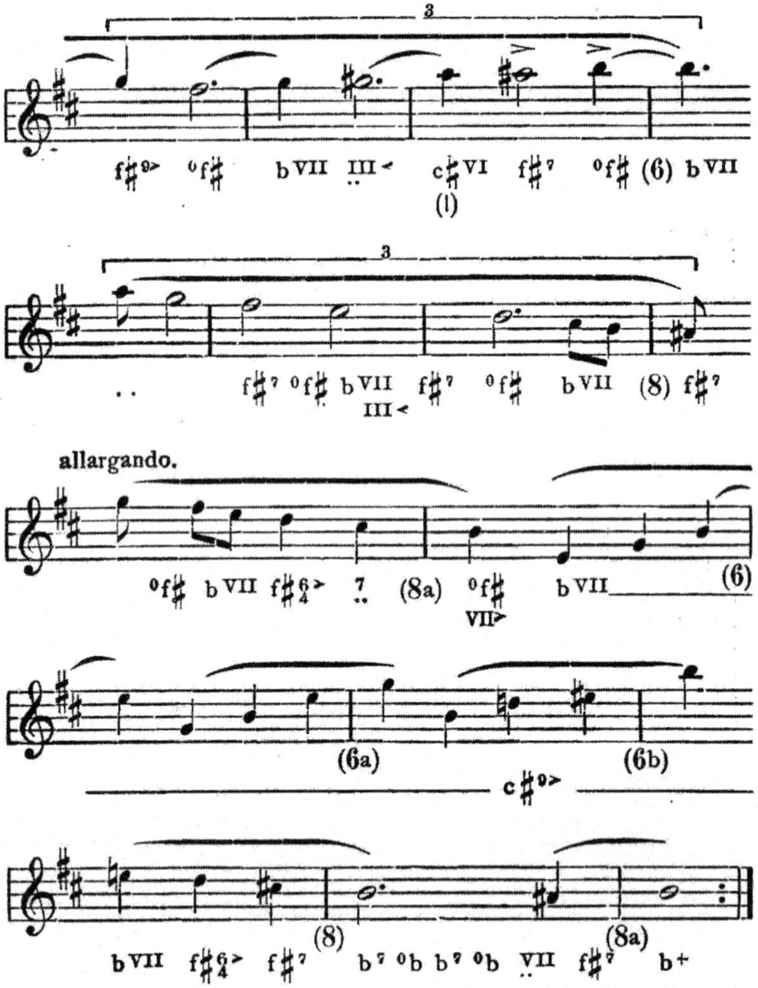

Here the figuration of the long extended $bVII$ displays boldnesses and hardnesses, greater than anything to be met with in the immediately following fugue. The passage, indeed, can be only understood, if the crossing over (leap from the changing note) be taken as ornament motive:

in place of

As the whole passage will permit the change to this simple, more easily intelligible kind of ornament, let me venture to take it as illustration, leaving out, at the same time, the passing notes in the bass which add to the difficulty

The last measure but one (NB) with the leap from the second upper-dominant ($c\sharp^{9>}$) to the chord of the Neapolitan sixth ($^{0}b^{2>}$) is still more striking. The passing note $f\sharp$ in the bass makes it much more difficult to understand the harmony; the quickest way of getting at the meaning is to put the simple under-dominant instead of the second upper-dominant, and write $c\sharp$ instead of c, for example:

Then does one become fully conscious of the double chromatic character ($c_{+}^{9>} = $ b$^{\overset{\text{VII}}{\text{III}}<}$, $c_+ = {}^{0}b^{2>}$, and likewise b^{VII}), and grasp the leap from the raised to the natural $\left(\begin{smallmatrix}\text{III}< \\ \text{V}>\end{smallmatrix} \text{---} \begin{smallmatrix}\text{III}\natural \\ \text{V}\natural\end{smallmatrix}\right)$, and from the natural (^{VII}) to the lowered notes ($^{\text{VII}>}$).

The fugue (à 4), considering the slow *tempo,* is probably the longest of the whole work. Spitta (Bach I. p 782; English edition Vol. 2. p. 176) says of the theme that it "proceeds slowly, sighing, saddened and pain-stricken", and finds in the whole fugue "the expression of suffering so intensified as to be almost unendurable", but bids one beware "of regarding the piercing bitterness of its effect as a mere result of a contrapuntal skill". He adds: — "From this point of view indeed it is in no way remarkable and even if it were, Bach has proved again and again that he could preserve a sweet and pleasing character even with the greatest intricacy of construction. No, it was his purpose to produce a picture of human misery, to give it full utterance here, in his favorite key, and at the close of this glorious work in which all his deepest sympathies with human feeling had found expression. For to live is to suffer." I cannot imagine that Bach "wished to produce a picture of human misery"; such a conception, besides, does not come within the limits of my other considerations. I may however say that the key of *B-minor,* the same in which Bach wrote his "Hohe Messe" and many other works of the highest importance, threw him into a state of inspired absorption so that he opened up his inmost soul, and told us of his griefs. But it is no ordinary grief, no feeble groaning and sighing, but a Faust-like search after truth, a true soul-struggle which reveals itself within these bold harmonic enclosures. The supposed uglinesses and intolerable hardnesses disappear entirely from the theme, and indeed from the whole fugue, as soon as one has gained a clear conception of the harmonies and of the metrical structure.

The theme — in which the upward - stretching steps of the prelude return in extended form, as more heartfelt, expressive movements — sinks first from the fifth of the key ($f\sharp$) to the third, in order next to soar upwards from the fundamental note to the sixth (g), and further, from the fifth ($f\sharp$) to the major seventh (with appoggiatura: b $a\natural$), but from here it sinks back to the third (with appoggiatura: e, $d\sharp$); the third is already raised, in the new intensified aspiration beyond the octave, first to the augmented octave (leading note of the dominant of the key of the dominant) whence it sinks back to the third of the second dominant, in order, finally, to seize as conqueror the octave ($d—c\sharp$), and from thence to glide quietly down to the fundamental note of the key of the dominant:

Let the following representation serve to make clear the harmonic succession

This exposition corresponds to the mode of writing
in my edition; the *c* written by Bach in the third measure
motive, is, however, intelligible as such, if it be taken as
ninth in *b*[7] — and then the third motive will sink back
to the under-dominant (⁰*b*); but the raising of the *e* to *e*♮,
and of the *g* to *g*♯ turns the under-dominant into the
second upper-dominant: —

    b*   (4)   ⁰b   c♯⁷   ⁰c♯

This exposition is all the happier in that it sets aside
the uncomfortably anticipated *b* before the fourth measure
(7th of *c*♯⁷). Perhaps, therefore, it would be better in this
case to restore Bach's original mode of writing (*c* instead
of *b*♮, and, further on, *f* instead of *e*♯ etc.). Anyhow either
method if carried out with full consciousness, and properly expressed in performance, eliminates from the theme
every unpleasantly sounding note. Besides it is of importance (and of this there is not sufficient hint in my edition),
that the major thirds which, in place of the expected minor harmonies appearing as resolutions of appoggiaturas

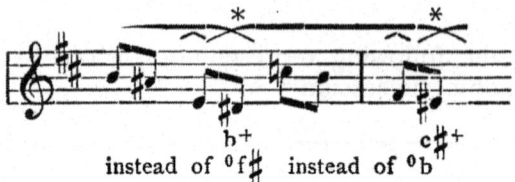

    instead of ⁰f♯   instead of ⁰b

should be somewhat emphasized, as they are not plain
end notes, but rather substitutes for end notes, notes which
lead onward, which induce modulation.

As the theme in its second half bears the stamp of
the key of the dominant, the answer must return from the
same to the principal key, which, as is known, is effected
by turning to the under-dominant side, *i. e.* by an answer
at the interval of a fourth.

This mode of answer enters, in fact, from the fifth
note, and is carried out strictly to the end. The answer-

ing of the $f\sharp$ at the commencement by b was, indeed, not absolutely necessary, and must probably be explained by the old household rules of fugal response, and by the habit of commencing the Comes with the fundamental tone when the Dux has commenced with the fifth (but which is only strictly logical when the Dux remains in the principal key, and the Comes by answering in the fifth would, against the rule, fall at once into the key of the dominant). If Bach's theme were only

the answer would have to be

The great extent of the theme and its firm modulation frees it altogether from this mode of answering, as it fails in its special aim, viz that of marking the principal key at the beginning. The harmonic meaning of the Comes, as already clearly established by the 1st countersubject, is as follows:

This first countersubject plays an important, and almost uninterrupted *rôle* throughout the whole fugue, though not unchanged throughout its whole extent; and, besides, its three chief motives *a*, *b* and *c* are frequently divided among several voices. The motive *a* and the ascending passage in *b* appear, already in the next theme entry, in inversion;

and indeed in the same voice (alto) in which the first theme entry and the first counterpoint were introduced; on the other hand the second voice (tenor) gives the remainder of the countersubject faithfully in direct motion. This division of the countersubject between two voices takes place again at the entry of the fourth voice between tenor and bass. The concluding motive (*d*) of the countersubject, which was already taken up in the short episode inserted between the 2nd and 3rd theme entries, is subjected to specially rich treatment. Here is the episode

The appended syncopated figure which alternates between the two voices, may be regarded as the germ of the long episode which occurs later on

The latter, however produce the effect of soothing balsam and gentle consolation in comparison with the powerfully pressing-forward of the original form, in which, resolutions by suspension, similar to those of the appogiatura notes in the theme, undergo chromatic change

From the second development the motive *a* of the first counterpoint assumes fresh importance, and, indeed, in its direct form, for it unfolds itself in a winding semiquaver passage

which, especially in the strettos (see below), assumes large dimensions.

The (syncopated) motive *c* of the first counterpoint, also acquires independent importance later on, and, indeed, in the refined form first hinted at in the second development

but which is only fully developed in its right place, the countersubject, in the concluding section

where it is preserved as a definite addition to the general wealth. The freedom with which Bach handles form here, is astonishing: those who assert that this fugue smells of the lamp and that it is principally occupied with contrapuntal combinations, have vision only surface-deep. The countersubject, as already mentioned, is treated very freely. Inversion, augmentation or diminution of the theme does not occur, nor are there even any real strettos, but, in place of the latter, many apparent strettos are forthcoming: —

Continuation freer

i. e. as soon as a new voice follows with the commencement of the theme, the old one gives it up — certainly no "midnight lamp" combination, but only easy handling of simple contrapuntal means. Quite original (one might be tempted to say humorous, were such an expression permissible in connection with this fugue) is the giving out — as if too soon — of the commencement of the theme, by a voice, which at once stops, but, four measures later, really introduces the theme: —

This occurs twice in the tenor at the beginning of the second development, likewise in *E-minor* two periods later.

I. *Exposition:* Dux in the alto, Comes in the tenor, after four free measures ♩ | ♩ Dux in the bass, and again, after two free ♩ | ♩ measures, Comes in the soprano. A long interlude (8 ♩ | ♩ measures) brings back the key,

which by a close-confirmation had been changed from
B-minor to *C♯-minor*, so that the tenor (after the early
entry already mentioned) by giving out the Dux in the principal key, marks a second development.

II. *Modulation Section.* After a long interlude (8 a,
8 b, 1—8, with the second premature tenor entry) the
tenor has the theme (Dux) in *E-minor* (closing in *B-minor*);
then, after two free measures, follows the first apparent stretto
between alto and soprano (the former in *F♯-minor*, the
latter in *B-minor*, not bringing the theme to an end, but
freely digressing, filling out the period, however, in regular
manner). Then comes the bass (again with the complete
theme, but with the opening step of the Comes (*e d*) in
B-minor, and — as a kind of confirmation of this complete development — an apparent stretto of the Dux
through all four voices (broken off at the second measure):
soprano (*B-minor*), alto (*E-minor*), bass (*A-major*), tenor
(*D-major*, fully carried out, hence closing in *A-major*).
But with that the master is not satisfied. The bass once
again starts in *A-major* (but as Comes), and concludes
with the complete theme in *D-major*; after six free measures (1—4, 3a—4a) the tenor enters with the Dux
in *F♯-minor*, leading to *C♯-minor*, from whence two inserted measures tend towards *E-major* (b⁷): the middle
section now closes with the Dux (once again in the Bass) in
E-major (instead of *E-minor*, chord of the Doric sixth) in
the direction of *B-minor*.

III. The *Closing-section* consists of four 8-measure
periods, the first of which has the Dux in *B-minor* given out by
the tenor, at the close of which in *F♯-minor* two acces-
sory measures (8 a, 8 b) turn to the half-close on *f♯⁷*,
whereupon an episode of eight measures marks the keys
of *D-major* and *B-minor*. The third period contains an
apparent stretto of the theme in *B-minor* and *E-minor*
between tenor and bass; the fourth, after two free measures, introduces once more the Dux in the alto (not coming quite to an end). Thus it may be seen that of the
supposed artificialities of the piece, truly little remains.
Whoever has rightly understood the theme, and thereby become capable of feeling, and making every note well-
sounding, will, without difficulty, find his way through the
whole fugue.

T/9/1922

MUSICAL TEXT BOOKS

IN

AUGENER'S EDITION

ENGLISH PRINTING & PAPER

		Net s. d.
9171	ALEXANDER, J. "Con Amore." Poetical Introduction to Musical Instruction	3 -
10123	ANTCLIFFE, H. The Successful Music Teacher. Second Impression	1 6
10124	How to Pass Music Examinations. The Successful Candidate. Words of Advice... ... ...Paper	1 6
10125	The Amateur Singer. Words of Advice	1 -
	BACH, J. S. Analysis of J. S. Bach's "48 Preludes and Fugues" (Wohltemperites Clavier). By Dr. H. Riemann. Fourth Impression :—	
9205	Part I. 24 Preludes and Fugues ... ... Bound	3 -
9206	Part II. 24 ,. Third Impression ... ... Bound	3 -
9210	BEETHOVEN PIANOFORTE SONATAS. Letters to a Lady, by Dr. C. Reinecke, translated by E. M. Trevenen Dawson	3 9
10091	CARSE, ADAM. Summary of the Elements of Music, with Exercises & Instructions on "How to Write Music"	1 6
10092	Key to the above	1 6
10093	Practical Hints on Orchestration	1 6
	CLARKE, J. A. Catechism of the Rudiments of Music. 384th Edition ... . Paper	1 6
	COCKING, F. The Composer's Vade Mecum. (English-Italian)	- 9
9215	CROKER, NORRIS. Handbook for Singers. Sixth Impression ... ... Bound	3 -
9199	DANNREUTHER, E. Wagner and the Reform of the Opera ... ... Bound with Portrait	6 -
10097	DAUGHTRY, O. Ear-Tests and How to prepare for Them. Fourth Impression	2 3
	EVETTS, EDGAR T. The Vocal Student's Practice Register with Vocabulary	- 9
	Modulator for use of Students of the Numeral and Rhythmic Methods (Vocal)	1 6
9179	GOODWIN, A. Practical Hints on the Technique and Touch of Pianoforte Playing. With Illustrations. Fourth Impression ... ... Bound	3 -
	HAMILTON. Dictionary of Musical Terms. Bound 2/3	1 6
10112	HEALE, H. A Short Treatise on the Rudiments of Music. 16mo.	- 9

PRACTICE RECORD and Mark Register for Music Pupils. Arranged for three terms 1 6

The same, arranged for one term ... ... - 9

10116 **POCHHAMMER, A.** Popular Handbook of Musical Informat on. (H. Heale) ... ...Bound 4 -

PROUT, PROF. EBENEZER :—

9182 Harmony: Its Theory and Practice. Thirty - ninth Impression ... ...Bound 7 6

9182e Analytical Key to the Exercises in the same. Fifth Impression ... .Bound 6 -

9183 Counterpoint: Strict and Free. Eleventh Impression. Bound 7 6

9183a Additional Exercises to " Counterpoint " with Melodies and Unfigured Basses for harmonizing. Eighth Impression... ... ...Bound 3 6

9184 Double Counterpoint and Canon. Fifth Impression. Bound 7 6

9185 Fugue. Seventh Impression ... ...Bound 7 6

9186 Fugal Analysis. Fourth Impression... ... ...Bound 7 6

9187 Musical Form. Tenth Impression ... ...Bound 7 6

9188 Applied Forms. Eighth Impression .. ..Bound 7 6

The Orchestra :

9189 I. Technique of the Instruments. Seventh Impression. Bound 7 6

9190 II. Orchestral Combination. Seventh Impression. Bound 7 6

9181 **PROUT, LOUIS B.** Harmonic Analysis. Second Edition 3 -

10106 Sidelights on Harmony ... ... 3 -

10107 Time, Rhythm and Expression. Second Impression ... - 9

9210 **REINECKE, C.** The Beethoven Pianoforte Sonatas. Letters to a Lady. Translated by E. M. Trevenen Dawson 3 9

9198 **RIEMANN, Dr. H.** Harmony Simplified; or the Theory of the Tonal Functions of Chords. Trans. from the German. Second Impression ... ...Bound 6 -

10115 L'Harmonie simplifiée, ou Théorie des fonctions tonales des accords. Translated by Prof. Georges Humbert ... 4 6

9201 Catechism of Musical Instruments (Guide to Instrumentation). Third Impression ... ...Bound 3 -

Catechism of Musical History :—

9202 Part I. History of Musical Instruments, and Hist ry of Tone Systems and Notations. Third Impression. Bound 3 -

9203 Part II. History of Musical Form, with Biographical Notices. Third Impression ... ...Bound 3 -

9204 Catechism of Pianoforte Playing. Third Impression. Bound 3 -

9207 Catechism of Musical Æsthetics. Second Impression. Bound 3 -

9209 Catechism of Orchestration ... ...Bound 3 -

9208 Introduction to playing from Score ... ...Bound 3 -

AUGENER Ltd.

18 GREAT MARLBOROUGH St.,
63 CONDUIT St. (Regent St. Corner) & 57 HIGH St., MARYLEBONE,
LONDON, W. I.

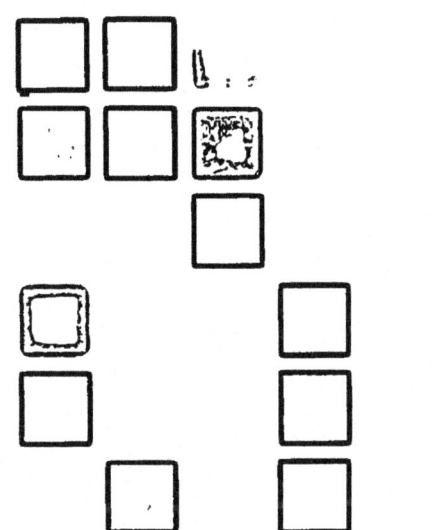

CPSIA information can be obtained
at www.ICGtesting.com
Printed in the USA
BVOW06*1857141216
470829BV00007B/22/P